I0235299

Edward Shaw of Boston

Antebellum Architect and Author—An Introduction

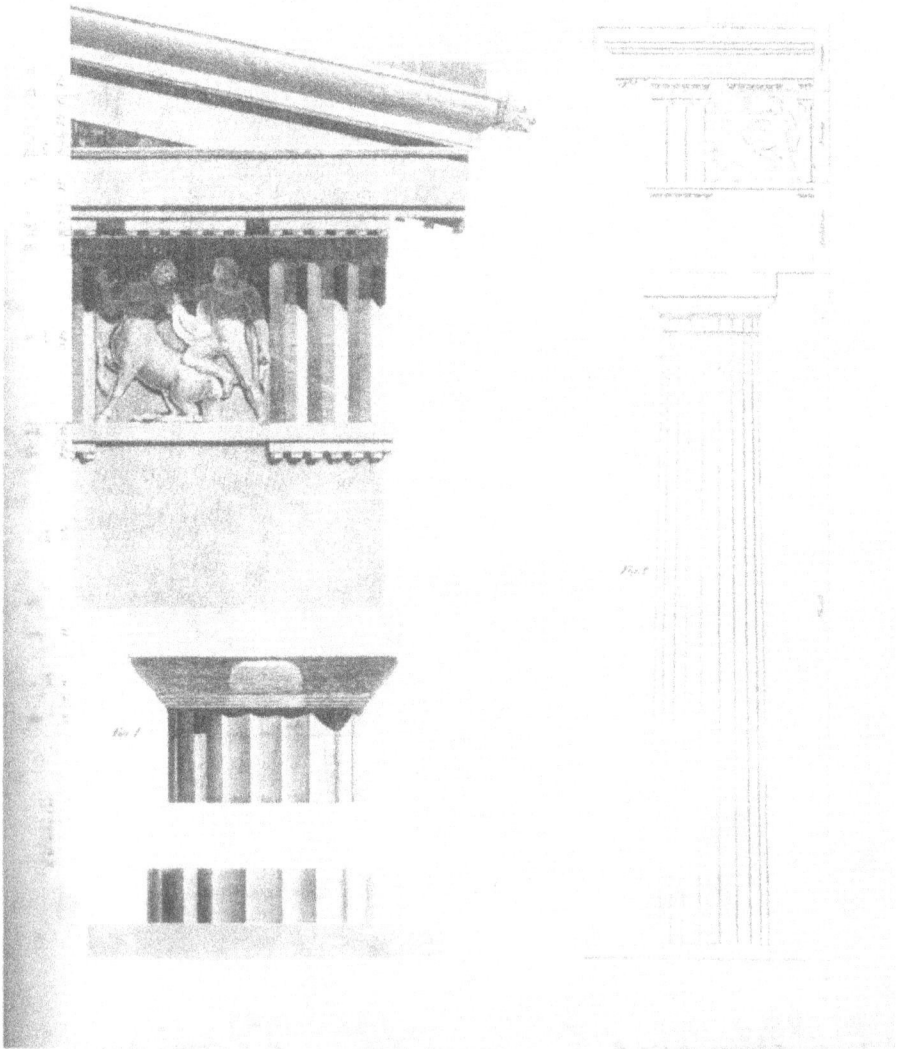

Edward Shaw, Grecian Doric from the Temple of Minerva at Athens, Plate 36 of the second edition of *Civil Architecture* (1832) as modified by Silloway and Harding for plate 44 of the sixth edition (1852). Author's collection.

Edward Shaw of Boston

Antebellum Architect and Author—An Introduction

James F. O'Gorman

American Philosophical Society Press
Philadelphia • 2016

Transactions of the
American Philosophical Society
Held at Philadelphia
For Promoting Useful Knowledge
Volume 106, Part 2

Copyright © 2016 by the American Philosophical Society for its Transactions series.

All rights reserved.

ISBN: 978-1-60618-062-4

U.S. ISSN: 0065-9746

Library of Congress Cataloging-in-Publication Data

Names: O'Gorman, James F., author.
Title: Edward Shaw of Boston : antebellum architect and author : an introduction /
James F. O'Gorman.
Description: Philadelphia, PA : American Philosophical Society Press, 2016. |
    Series: Transactions of the American Philosophical Society, ISSN 0065-9746 ;
    volume 106, part 2 | Includes bibliographical references and index.
Identifiers: LCCN 2016030292 | ISBN 9781606180624 (alk. paper)
Subjects: LCSH: Shaw, Edward, 1784- | Shaw, Edward, 1784—-Written works.
Classification: LCC NA737.S455 O39 2016 | DDC 720.92—dc23
LC record available at https://lccn.loc.gov/2016030292

To the memory of Ernest Allen Connally, who inspired me to become a historian of architecture and, in 1960, set my inaugural task as the study of the Western literature on the subject. It was then that I first perused Edward Shaw's *The Modern Architect.*

The book will outlive the building.
                    —Lars Müller

Contents

Preface

The study of nineteenth-century American architecture has proceeded without all the facts necessary to comprehend the subject fully. And, for that reason, it has been unbalanced. It did not begin with the end of the Civil War, the return of Richard Morris Hunt and H. H. Richardson from France, the opening of the school of architecture at Massachusetts Institute of Technology, the innovations in engineering that led to the skyscraper, and so on, subjects that have been well scoured in the search for the origins of so-called Modernism, but the emphasis of scholarship on the post-Civil War years might lead one to think so. The century's foundation was laid well before that conflict although it is difficult to see that clearly from recent published studies with the exception of W. Barksdale Maynard's fine selective survey of *Architecture in the United States, 1800–1850* (2002). What works exist for the early period have been spotty. A scan of monographs on the architects of the early years, for example, reveals an elitist approach to the subject. There are published studies of the careers of Benjamin Henry Latrobe, Thomas Jefferson, Robert Mills, and Alexander Jackson Davis, but none (although there are scattered articles, and some doctoral dissertations sit in archives) on Asher Benjamin, Ithiel Town, John Haviland, James Bogardus, John Notman, Alexander Parris, and others. The monographs we have on Samuel Sloan, William Strickland, Richard Upjohn, James Renwick, and others are woefully out of date. There is some slight indication that this might be changing, however. Jhennifer Amundson has T. U. Walter well in hand; I have in recent years looked behind the ample figure of H. H. Richardson and the startling works of Frank Furness to produce monographs on Hammatt Billings, Gervase Wheeler, Henry Austin, and Isaiah Rogers. The careers of these and other men of the period formed the cornerstone of the profession. And with this study I introduce a not entirely fully rounded profile of Edward Shaw of Boston. Perhaps other scholars will again discover the antebellum years, and we shall at last have a comprehensive architectural history of the century from beginning to end.

Known facts about the career of Edward Shaw are not now sufficiently available for a definitive monograph, and may never be; the following is, rather, a research source for further study. Brought together here are scattered bits of biographical, architectural, and literary information, materials toward such a monograph, plus some generalizations about Shaw's place in antebellum American architecture as can be deduced from the information in hand. Although his built achievement is slight and little known, there are several sets of drawings for commissions and competitions that survive. The broad distribution of his publications—themselves noticed but little studied—placed him at the center of the early development of the literature of architecture in this country. My approach combines the history of architecture with the history of the book. Although few of the buildings Shaw designed and saw erected survive, copies of his books, in their many editions, await thorough analysis in numerous school and public as well as private libraries across the land, online at the Digital Public Library of America and other such sites, in microfiche in the Library of American Civilization, or for sale through eBay or Bookfinder.com for antiquarian examples and modern reprints, and many other sources.

Acknowledgments

A book, even as concise a one as this, is never the work of the author alone. Earle G. Shettleworth, Jr. jump-started it, as he has with so many books, with an enormous amount of research. Special thanks also go to Catherine W. Bishir, Maggie DeVries, Jeanne Hablanian, Lauren Hewes, Michael J. Lewis, Michael Winship, and Charles B. Wood III.

Others who contributed in various ways, including leafing through volumes in their collections, were Sarah Allaback of the Library of American Landscape History; Jenifer Baker at North Carolina State University; Jennifer Betts at the Hay Library, Brown University; Richard J. and Carol Betts of the University of Illinois; Joanne Bloom, Fine Arts Library, Harvard University; Megan Bresnahan, Tisch Library, Tufts University; Harry Clark; Ethan Carr of the University of Massachusetts; Margaret Culbertson of the Bayou Bend Collection; Kathleen Curran of Trinity College; Jessica Hoppe Dagci at the Marquand Library of Art and Archaeology, Princeton University; Edwin Deegan, Fisher Fine Arts Library, University of Pennsylvania; Mary Beth Derrick at the University of Virginia; Sally S. Dickinson of the Trinity College Library; Lindsay Elgin at the Hay Library, Brown University; Caitlin Emory at Old Sturbridge Village; Prof. Peter Fergusson of Wellesley College; Nicholas Fry at the St. Louis Mercantile Library; Theodore Gantz and Heather Hope Gendron, Sloane Art Library, University of North Carolina; Laurin Christa Goad; Jordan Gofflin, Providence Public Library; Vincent Golden at the American Antiquarian Society; Laura K. Graveline, Rauner Library, Dartmouth College; Linda P. Gross, Hagley Museum; Jacquelyn Groves, University of Nebraska—Lincoln; Emily Guthrie, Winterthur; Kenneth Hafertepe of Baylor University; Teresa M. Harris, Avery Library, Columbia University; Kim Hoagland, Michigan Technological University; Joel Hollander, Guilford Connecticut; A. K. Houghland, Michigan Technical University; Robert Kelly, Redwood Library; Pat Larabee, Maine Charitable Mechanic Association; Margot K. Lystra; Lorrie McAllister of the Rotch Library at Massachusetts Institute of Technology; Alan Michelson, University of Washington; Deborah Mongeau, University of Rhode Island Library; Christopher P. Monkhouse; Cindy Morawski, Fitchburg Public Library; J. B. Muns Fine Arts Books; the late Denys Peter

Myers; Stephen C. Nedell of the Malden Public Library; Lena Newman of the Avery Library; Nicholas Noyes at the Maine Historical Society; Jaclyn Penny of the American Antiquarian Society; Roger G. Reed of the National Register of Historic Places; Deborah Richards in the Mt. Holyoke College Archive; Ruth Rogers, Clapp Library, Wellesley College; Robert Saarnio of the University of Mississippi; Meredith Santaus; Carly Sentieri, Miami of Ohio; Joel Silver and Zachary Downey of the Lilly Library, Indiana University; Catherina Slautterback of the Boston Athenaeum; Lee Sorensen, Lilly Library, Duke University; Kim Steinsiek of Duttenhofer's Books; Vaughn Stewart at Duke University; Lisa Struthers of the San Jacinto Museum; Sandra Tatman of the Athenaeum of Philadelphia; George E. Thomas of Philadelphia; Renée Tribert of the Connecticut Trust; David Van Zanten at Northwestern University; Angelo Vigorito of the General Society of Mechanics & Tradesmen in the City of New York; Robert Volz and Elaine Yanow at the Williams College Library; Anita Weaver, The Huntington Library; Krista White of Rutgers; Christopher Wigren of the Connecticut Trust; Richard Guy Wilson at the University of Virginia; and Joseph Wright, Sherman Library, Dartmouth College. I thank them one and all.

Once again I am most happy to recognize the primary importance of a Faculty Research Grant from Wellesley College as well as a Franklin Research Grant from the American Philosophical Society. I am heartily grateful for their continuing support of my efforts to light candles in dark corners.

List of Illustrations

Front cover: Town House (now part of City Hall), Manchester, New Hampshire, 1844–45. Vintage postcard courtesy of Earle G. Shettleworth, Jr.

Frontispiece: Edward Shaw, Grecian Doric from the Temple of Minerva at Athens. Plate 36 of the second edition of *Civil Architecture* (1832) as modified by Silloway and Harding for plate 44 of the sixth edition (1852).

1

BOSTON

E dward Shaw arrived in Boston as an experienced housewright in the early
1820s, just as the Anglophile, Roman-based, delicate brick-and-wooden
architecture of the Federal-era town was beginning to give way to the
Greek-based, heavy granite classicism of the early nineteenth-century city. The
most respected architect of the previous period, Charles Bulfinch, was away in
Washington supervising work on the national Capitol although his local influence
lingered. Others of that generation include Peter Banner and Asher Benjamin,
the latter the author of a number of influential books reaching in many editions
just past midcentury.[1] Leading architects of the second quarter of the century
were a group of mutually friendly men that included Alexander Parris, Solomon
Willard, Isaiah Rogers, and Ammi B. Young. Like Shaw, all had come from
outside the city, and had emerged from the building trades. From the 1820s on
they appropriated the granite emerging from the quarries at Quincy to produce
such large neoclassical landmarks as St. Paul's Cathedral, the branch Bank of
the United States, Tremont House, U. S. Custom House, and other imposing
works.[2] With at least two exceptions, Shaw's realized buildings merged with those
of a group of now less remembered names, including John Kutts,[3] Cornelius
Coolidge,[4] Charles (C. G.) Hall,[5] and William Sparrell.[6] None of them is now
thought of as having created memorable, monumental works. Were it not for
Shaw's books, and his landmark Thaxter House on Beacon Hill, his place in
Boston's architectural history would be as obscure as theirs. Buildings erected
from Shaw's drawings are now scarce and, in fact, may always have been. There
are more of his drawings to study than of his standing buildings to visit. His
reputation must now rest largely on his books, which, in subsequent editions and
reprints, outlasted even those now-better-remembered ones of Benjamin, and
contributed importantly to the history of nineteenth-century architecture and
architectural publication in America.[7]

When Shaw arrived in Boston he first joined the ranks of men like Cornelius
Coolidge or Jesse Shaw (of no proven relationship) who were busy up on Beacon
Hill, and young Isaiah Rogers, still a builder trained by Jesse Shaw but soon to
become a major Granite-Style architect under the tutelage of Solomon Willard.[8]
A much later report that stems from Thomas W. Silloway, an architect born in
1828 who was to help significantly "revise and improve" the sixth edition of
Shaw's Civil Architecture of 1852, names Peter Banner as Shaw's main tutor.
According to Silloway, who emphasized that he had known Shaw personally, "Mr.
Shaw was a pupil of Mr. Banner, and later took up Mr. Banner's practice."[9] Also,
according to the same source, Shaw had in his possession an original drawing
of the Park Street Church, Banner's major work of 1809. Although no documents
have appeared to reinforce this claim, the chronology fits. If Banner did train
Shaw, it was between the latter's arrival in the city about 1822 and Banner's
disappearance from known sources after 1828, when Shaw first styled himself
an architect.

Peter Banner's career in this country exemplifies the path taken by many of his local peers, including Shaw, an outsider who moved from London to New York to New Haven to Boston while describing himself as a builder and surveyor ("who designs and executes buildings of any description"), then architect and builder, and finally simply architect.[10] However scarcely documented all this is, it is highly characteristic of the architectural scene in Boston and elsewhere along the Eastern seaboard in the early nineteenth century. Banner's work followed the older tradition of wood-and-brick architecture, and so, in the main, did Shaw's. Unlike Rogers, Shaw proved generally inept at designing large stone buildings despite publishing two versions of a book on masonry materials and construction. With, perhaps, directions in drawing, especially the orders, from Banner (the housewright presumably needing little instruction in practical techniques), plus his early experience erecting buildings with or without his own sketches, with surely some access to English and American books on architecture as well as those of the European masters in translation, and acquaintanceship with some learned Bostonians, Shaw was ready by the late 1820s to find a place within the architectural world of the Hub and to lay out his first book.

Basic biographical facts are thin; no portrait of the man is known. Aside from a few documents associated with his Thaxter house, little manuscript material has survived for use in this study. We do know that Edward Shaw was born in North Hampton, on the New Hampshire coast south of Portsmouth, on August 2, 1784, the oldest of the eight children conceived by John and Molly Dustin Shaw. In 1790 the family moved northwest to nearby Sanbornton where Edward eventually became a carpenter's apprentice. His was a family of builders: Brother Benjamin (1794–1883) was a carpenter who early settled in Jackson, Michigan; brother David was a lumber merchant who built his own house in Sanbornton; brother John was a mason in the Merrimack River region. Certainly early on Edward shared techniques with his siblings. That he later published works on masonry materials and construction, in part the "result of many years of practical experience and personal observation," as he wrote, suggests that he also worked in that trade. He married Mary Abrams in 1808 and moved to New Chester (now Hill), New Hampshire, due west of Portland, Maine, where he worked as a builder until moving to Boston, some hundred miles to the southeast.[11]

Edward Shaw is last listed as an architect in the city directory for 1846–47; his latest known local building project is dated 1849. He signed the introductory material in his books through the sixth edition of *Civil Architecture* issued in 1852, but since the latter introduction is dated on the first day of the year of publication, his work on the book must have ended in 1851. And, in fact, it would appear that Silloway and Harding, signing themselves "The Editors," added much new material and rearranged the organization of that edition. Shaw's last title, *The Modern Architect*, which appeared in 1854 (although, as we shall see, there seems to have been advanced copies by mid-1853) was largely a reworking of his *Rural Architecture* of 1843, and it contains a "Publisher's Preface" dated 1854 that was probably not written by Shaw. His name does appear as signee of a footnote to that preface dated May 15, 1854, but that footnote was originally printed on paper different from that of the book's pages and tipped into some copies of the 1854 edition. It became integral to the letterpress only in some later editions. So it would seem that his active career ended (and he left town) somewhere between late 1851 and early 1854. He died in Chester, New Hampshire, in 1859. In some three decades in Boston he is listed at fifteen different addresses, which, if they do not all represent working offices rather than residences, might indicate that he never earned enough to buy himself a "dwelling-house," although he designed many for others. He seems to have stood outside the ranks of preferred Boston designers.[12] He "met with rebuff in attempts for the patronage of the city government," according to one source.[13] By contrast, his local, older competitor as author of architectural books, Asher Benjamin, served briefly on the Board of Aldermen in the 1820s.

Shaw lived through the period when most American-born architects began their careers as "mechanics," as carpenters or masons. In the 1831 edition of *Civil Architecture* he mentions his twenty years of practice. In the Preface to his *Rural Architecture* of 1843, he mentions his more than thirty years of experience as a practical builder. In his 1854 footnote to the Publishers' Preface in *The Modern Architect*, in answer to questions about his practical knowledge of carpentry and joinery, he was a bit more detailed. He wrote that he had "served in that capacity twenty years—fourteen of which, as contractor and builder, drawing all of my own plans and designs for private and public dwellings costing from five hundred to forty thousand dollars each. Since that time I have spent fifteen years in the theoretical practice and science of Architectural Drawings and Plans, both ancient and modern." Although this might have been in part an attempt to reassure his readers that he knew what he was doing, it seems also a late, and somewhat foggy, indication of how he saw his career.

His tally of the years is rough; his description of it needs parsing.[14] In the first two tellings, he traced his career back to the 1810s. In the latter case he divided it into two unequal parts. He contrasts his activity during the immediately precedent fifteen years, thus his career since the late 1830s, to the previous twenty, for only fourteen of which he designed and erected a variety of building types. For his time as a contractor he gives a cost range of his projects. As even the spotty catalogue of his known local buildings, executed or proposed, stretches from the 1820s through the 1840s, and we have architectural drawings dated during all of this time and know he supervised construction up to the last, we must wonder why he erroneously divided his later career into two vaguely defined parts: first as practitioner then as a theoretician.

The distinction might lie not in chronology or draftsmanship, but in the words *ancient* and *modern*, which seem to refer to a study of the classical orders and their use in contemporary buildings. But that began as early as his first book in the late 1820s, not, as he suggests, about 1840. It seems he wanted to distinguish his building career from his publishing career rather than give an accurate, chronological accounting of his development or merely prove he was an experienced woodworker in answer to the questions that apparently generated his remarks. In so doing he rather vaguely outlined what it took for a mechanic to become an architect. In his scheme of things, it seems, one needed to draw but one also needed time with the books as well as on the job in order to reach the more lofty title. Two of his books addressed practical issues of construction, whereas three others emphasized a more theoretical approach to the "science." It seems that Shaw's intention in writing that footnote was not only to reassure his readers or to create a timeline, but to describe a recipe for success and pass it on to the readership of *The Modern Architect,* a book subtitled *Every Carpenter his Own Master.*

Shaw's books are copiously illustrated with copperplate engravings by several artists, including William W. Wilson, a Bostonian who, from the 1830s on, turned out bank notes, safety checks, bills of exchange, and so forth.[15] His frontispiece to Shaw's 1854 book (Figure 1) depicts a domestic construction site in which workers in the background raise a barn adjacent to a two-story gabled Italianate house with piazza, in front of which stand diminutive figures of, perhaps, owners or gawkers (one is a child). In the foreground, an architect, clad in top hat, frock coat, and spats, with dividers and rule in hand and a sheaf of drawings at his feet, explains his drafted ideas to two mechanics, heads uncovered and coatless, while a third, in shirt sleeves, rips a board with a hand saw. (Other carpenters' tools are in evidence in a box behind the architect: folding rule, hand auger with spare bits, and an ax. A still life arrangement of others, comprised of a square, tape holder, hammer, and adjustable carpenter's dividers, lies in the immediate foreground.[16]) The status of the actors is indicated by their habiliment: the well-dressed architect directs the design, the produce of his intellect, while the unfrocked men work with their hands to execute his directions. It has been said that the work on the barn is the earliest depiction of the balloon frame, an assertion that has been challenged by Ted Cavanagh.[17] Be that as it may, the real value of the scene, whose iconology was surely dictated by Shaw, is its representation of a professional architect, a man who had evolved from a housewright over the previous half century to become the person who gives rather than takes orders at the building site. Although the subtitle of the book promises it will make "every carpenter his own master," Wilson's frontispiece makes clear that Shaw did not mean "master carpenter" but the separation of the roles of builder and designer. This contrasts sharply with their continued melding in the

Figure 1 William W. Wilson, Engraver & Printer, Frontispiece to Edward Shaw, *The Modern Architect*, Dayton & Wentworth, 1854, Author's collection.

titles of books by Asher Benjamin, such as *The Architect, or Practical House Carpenter*, reissued into the 1850s.[18]

Assuming that small-town New Hampshire in the last years of the eighteenth century was not a hot bed of intellectual resources—that books on the subject of architecture and related topics were few and far between in that era and area—we would probably not be wrong to guess that Shaw acquired his knowledge of the theory—if not the practice—of his profession after he arrived in Boston. (It is beyond thinking that he ever traveled abroad, although he writes about English and continental buildings and quotes foreign sources.) It is not clear how he accomplished this, but speculation produces some suggestions. Boston was well stocked with all manner of applicable books when Shaw arrived, including those at the recently formed Mechanic Apprentices' Library Association. In his publications he cites (and copies from) an astonishingly broad range of general texts, a range significantly more numerous than what we find cited or quoted in the publications of Asher Benjamin or those of Shaw's other competitors in book production, the kinds of titles that are listed, for example, in the 1838 catalogue of the Apprentices' Library.[19] Although Shaw was not an apprentice when he arrived, it must be assumed that there were ways of finding books for an ambitious man, for his texts quote so many. The few established architects (such as Charles Bulfinch and Alexander Parris), and some of their clients, surely had personal libraries of architectural books, however small. The proprietary Architectural Library of Boston was founded in 1809.[20] By the time Shaw arrived in the city, its collection had been taken over by the Associated Housewright Society led by Parris.[21] In his transition from mechanic to architect, Shaw may have had the help of not only Banner but Parris, with whom he briefly shared an address on Popular Street; perhaps through Parris he had access to the books from that library.

The title page of his first book, *Civil Architecture*, written during the last years of the 1820s, lists the then much-cited standard works by "Vitruvius, Stuart, Chambers, and Nicholson" as the sources of his discussion of the classical orders, but he who was, even more than his competitors, a "compiler," would copy passages from many more authorities in this and later books. Latin and Italian versions of Vitruvius could be found at Harvard in the late eighteenth century. That august institution was probably not open to housewrights, but translations and anthologies were also available.[22] For example, the *Rudiments of Ancient Architecture*, third edition, with extracts from Vitruvius, Pliny, and so on, which might have been available to him. Shaw does cite Henry Aldrich's well-illustrated *The Elements of Civil Architecture, According to Vitruvius and Other Ancients, and the Most Approved Practice of Modern Authors, Especially Palladio*, which appeared in a second edition in 1818 (reprinted 1824). He mentions it several times in his books. It contains, as do Shaw's texts, sections on architectural history from ancient Rome to the Renaissance, building techniques, parts of buildings from rooms to stairways, and the orders. James Stuart and Nicholas Revett's *Antiquities of Athens* must have existed locally in several copies. Isaiah Rogers, for example, cribbed from it in designing his famed Tremont House in 1827 (a building Shaw mentions in *Rural Architecture*). William Chambers's *A Treatise on the Decorative Parts of Civil Architecture* was at Harvard by 1790 and in its later editions must also have proven useful. It is unlikely that early on Shaw had access to many such collections of books, but by the time he began publishing, however, he did (and a possible source other than Parris will be mentioned below). He obviously had access to a number of critical or informative works in his field and beyond, or excerpts from those in anthologies. We shall look at this in more detail when we consider Shaw's several publications (see Chapter 3).

The range of subjects Shaw had perused by the end of the 1840s, as exemplified by both the texts and the illustrations in his books, closely resembles those of one of his chief sources, England's Peter Nicholson, a figure whose publications were well known in America and cited by Shaw, Asher Benjamin, and others. Even a partial list of the Britisher's many books shows a man of broad experience in carpentry (*The Carpenter's New Guide*, 1792), masonry (*Popular and Practical Treatise on Masonry and Stone-cutting*, 1827), stair building (*Treatise on the Construction of Staircases and Handrails*, 1820), mathematics (*Popular Course of Pure and Mixed Mathematics*, 1822), design (*Principles of Architecture*, 1795), and many more. In short, Nicholson treated his subject at the theoretical as well as the practical level, just as Shaw expressed his intention to do in the title of his *Civil Architecture*, which he describes as a "theoretical and practical system of building." Such broad knowledge would lead the mechanic to become his own master, as it is expressed in the subtitle to *The Modern Architect*, one who gives rather than takes orders at the building site. This knowledge came to Shaw from his perusal of a wide range of published works not only on architecture but science as well (see Appendix).

The four authorities Shaw lists on the title page of *Civil Architecture* far from account for all his sources. As will become apparent in the section on his books, there is reference to a large collection of English and Continental authorities. Some of these authorities are also mentioned in passing by his competitors, but at times Shaw's texts have an almost scholarly ring. There are, to give some full titles, works such as Roland Fréart de Chambray, *Parallèle de l'architecture antique avec la modern* (1650; English translations available); Sébastion Le Clerc, *Traité d'architecture* (1714; English translation 1723–24); Andrea Palladio, *I quattro libri dell'architettura* (in several English versions); Vincenzo Scamozzi, *L'Idea dell'architettura universale* (1615); Thomas Rickman, *An Attempt to Discriminate the Styles of English Architecture* (1819); Giacomo Barozzi da Vignola, *Regola delli cinque ordini d'architettura* (1563; at Harvard by 1765); and, as we shall see, there were others, and not all of them architectural publications. He also refers to the *Gentleman's Magazine*, for example, a monthly that carried news and commentary on a broad range of topics that appealed to the literate public. Of course the question remains, how did Shaw gain access to any of these sources? Where did he find all his information? How could he use the ones in foreign languages? Less likely from the originals just listed, perhaps, than from compendia such as Henry Aldrich's.

As we know, Shaw's evolution from carpenter and mason to architect, from hammer and trowel to straight edge and drafting pen, followed one common path for early nineteenth-century designers in this country. This is witnessed in the changing titles of books on architecture published by Asher Benjamin prior to Shaw's first book. Benjamin's titles shift from *The Country Builder's Assistant* of 1797 to his *The Rudiments of Architecture* of 1814. Seven home-grown builder's guides preceded Shaw's first, including four by Benjamin and one each by Owen Biddle, John Haviland (a British immigrant), and Minard Lafever.[23] Only one of the seven contains the word *architecture* in its title.

The first of those, Benjamin's *The Country Builder's Assistant*, a small (duodecimo) collection of plates of details with brief descriptions, was based largely on Chambers and Nicholson. It contained two domestic designs and one ecclesiastical scheme shown, as was common, in plan and elevation. Owen Biddle's quarto, *The Young Carpenter's Assistant, or A System of Architecture, Adapted to the Style of Building in the United States* appeared in Philadelphia in 1805 and is listed in the catalogue of the Boston Architectural Library in 1809. His titular patriotic reference was imitated by Benjamin in his next book, and eventually by Shaw in the 1843 edition of his *Rural Architecture . . . Designed for the United States of America*. Biddle, a Philadelphian, also sought guidance in the older literature, especially English, as did those who followed him, including Shaw. His book was a step beyond Benjamin's first effort. Introducing himself as a "House Carpenter and Teacher of Architectural Drawing," he begins with the drawing board and T-square, proceeds through geometry, and discusses the orders, architectural details, and designs for an urban dwelling. He modifies Palladio's instructions using his own experience. He introduced a dictionary of building terminology Shaw would expand in his own glossaries.[24]

Benjamin's *The American Builder's Companion* of 1806 appeared in its sixth and last edition in 1827 or about the time Shaw began to plan his *Civil Architecture*. It ranges from "practical geometry"; a brief notice on the "Origin of Building" in which Indian wigwams are mentioned and Vitruvius, Chambers, and Nicholson cited; Roman then Greek orders with all their decorative parts described, with mention of Sebastiano Serlio and Roland Fréart de Chambray; doors, windows, and stairs discussed; designs given for dwellings (including the "practical parts": a kitchen with Rumford stove) and for a courthouse, meeting houses, and churches, all illustrated. Shaw's *Civil Architecture* would cover some of the same territory. His title page mentions the same authorities as Benjamin. He discusses history at greater length and, as we have noted, cites many more authorities. But in this, his first book, he offered no complete prototypical building designs, as did Benjamin.

The Builder's Assistant of 1818–21 by John Haviland of Philadelphia, a British-trained professional, was a house pattern book that included both Roman and Greek orders. Shaw was to quote verbatim from it. The last two books are contemporary with Shaw's first. Minard Lafever's *The Young Builder's General*

Instructor appeared in 1829 (when Shaw was certainly far along on his first endeavor). A New Yorker, a younger contemporary of Shaw, and like him a carpenter turned architect (the men entered the profession at much the same time; each launched his architectural career with a book as well as a building), Lafever included some of the same territory as his predecessors, expressed his indebtedness to Nicholson, but eventually was himself not satisfied with the result.[25] In 1833 he published the first edition of his *Modern Builder's Guide*. His Preface again singles out Nicholson as his main source, and Stuart for the architectural orders. He proceeds from "Geometry Adapted to Practical Carpentry"; to "Practical Stair Railing"; "Grecian Architecture" (quoting "Stewart" at great length); window shutters; "Terms Used in Carpentry and Joinery" (quoted from Nicholson); "Ornamental Masonry"; "Terms, and ... Tools Used in Masonry," including mortars; "Plastering," in which he mentions James Wyatt on stucco and "Scagliola," a composition that Shaw did not discuss until his *Practical Masonry* of 1846; and finally a "Glossary of Technical Terms" taken from Nicholson. Lafever, even more than his peers, quoted extensively from the publications of others. His *The Beauties of Modern Architecture* of 1835 contains 48 (handsome) plates, a glossary taken from the *Encyclopaedia Britannica*, and a sixty-three-page extract on architectural history lifted verbatim from "Elme's Dictionary," that is, James Elmes's *Lectures on Architecture* of 1823. The works of Benjamin and Lafever especially jostled for attention with those of Shaw in ads announcing their books in the local press.

Asher Benjamin's *The Practical House Carpenter: Being a Complete Development of the Grecian Orders* of 1830 appeared at the same time as *Civil Architecture*. It reflected the triumph of Greek precedent over the last fifteen years. Shaw too offered plates on both Roman and Greek orders. We find the word *practical* (and its variant, *operative*) used over and over again in this period, applied to the architects themselves and to both the character of their books and their contents. It seems to have been a popular "Madison Avenue" word, reassuring to potential users and their clients. Shaw presumably had access to many or all of his contemporaries' publications. What he thought about them is not on record, although he did copy from them and other sources, often verbatim.

And, as Shaw included two plates of chimney pieces after Isaiah Rogers's designs for Boston's Tremont Hotel in his *Civil Architecture*, he certainly knew one other local architectural publication, the *Description of the Tremont House* of 1830, written anonymously by William H. Eliot. But as a monograph on a single building, the first of its kind in this country, it could have had little other influence on Shaw's own book.[26]

So Shaw's *Civil Architecture* was as a whole no revolutionary American publication. His history might have been more extensive, his discussion of building systems more detailed, his glossaries of architectural and technical terms more complete than those of his countrymen, but his approach and coverage in the main reflected those of his predecessors. What do stand out in the context of previous American books are his range of named and unnamed sources,[27] and his discussion of design using perspective projection and shadows. The latter was a topic then unprecedented in the architectural literature of this country although as old as Vignola (whom Shaw mentions) and as recent as Peter Nicholson's *The Rudiments of Practical Perspective* (1822) and Joseph Gwilt's *Sciography, or Examples of Shadows* (1822). He also included an early discussion in this country in the context of architecture of wood and iron bridge construction, including the work of Ithiel Town. And none of the works by Shaw's contemporaries include the kind of detailed treatment of masonry materials and construction based upon historical research that he produced in his *Operative Masonry* and its sequel, *Practical Masonry*. On this subject he had no peer among architect-written books during his lifetime.

His subsequent books would vary from his first title by de-empathizing mathematics and emphasizing model house and church designs. But it was not until 1843 that he introduced his own ecclesiastical designs and perspective representations of his domestic work, and in the latter, as we shall see, his presentation was completely outclassed by the contemporary publications of A. J. Davis, A. J. Downing, and others.

Somewhat later American books available in Boston that might be thought of as competitors to Shaw's original output (excluding Benjam in's *The Practice of Architecture* [1833] and *The Builder's Guide* [1839], which rely on that author's earlier books) include Chester Hills's *The Builder's Guide*, which appeared at Hartford in 1834, with a revised edition of 1846 repeated in 1847, and William Brown's *The Carpenter's Assistant* issued in Boston and several other places in 1848, with more editions to 1856. Biographical details of either author are not available (although according to Hitchcock's *American Architectural Books*, Brown hailed from Lowell, Massachusetts, and a William Brown is listed as a mason in the *Lowell Directory* for 1847). Hills's is a "practical treatise," as his title tells us, containing the orders, the Gothic style of building (with details from Augustus Charles Pugin's *Specimens of Gothic Architecture* of 1821–23, a standard source), carpentry, masonry, and so on, "adapted to the wants of the less experienced," all illustrated with thirty-four lithographed plates. By 1851, when Brown had had the advantage of consulting books by A. J. Davis, A. J. Downing, Gervase Wheeler, and William Bailey Lang, in his fourth edition he credited to Lewis E. Joy of Worcester, Massachusetts, the designs for rural cottages, villas, and farm buildings. The presentation of those designs reflected the arrival of the rendered picturesque cottage of the Davis–Downing collaboration, something Shaw did not follow in *The Modern Architect* of 1854. Brown's book stands midway between the builder's guides, aimed at the trade, and the emerging house pattern or "stylebooks" of the period, aimed at the public.[28] In other ways, however, his work is standard fare for a builder's guide: Egyptian, Grecian, and Roman styles, the orders, geometry, specifications, and a glossary.

The engraved plate illustrations in Shaw's last two architectural titles, his *Rural Architecture* of 1843 and its more or less reissue as *The Modern Architect* of 1854, some of them copied from Englishman Samuel Brooks's *Designs for Cottage and Villa Architecture* of 1839, are old fashioned when compared to— among other American works of these decades—Lewis Falley Allen's *Rural Architecture* of 1852 (reissued to 1865), Oliver P. Smith's *The Domestic Architect* of 1852 (reissued 1854), or Samuel Sloan's two-volume *The Model Architect* of 1852–53. Allen's work, unlike Shaw's *Rural Architecture*, did actually concern the rural. It was published by Orange Judd & Company of New York, the agricultural book publishers, and is a "complete description" of farmhouses and farm structures. Smith's work, first published in Buffalo and then in New York City, is a collection of designs aimed at the country builder rather than the "certain class of architects" served by existing publications, although his content seems to owe much to Shaw's earlier books. He gives the usual historical survey, designs for rural and ornamental cottages in the Grecian and Cottage styles, rules for building, a glossary, notes on heat and ventilation, directions for "drawing and shading, and the rudiments of linear perspective" (following Shaw's lead), as well as directions to the builder. His perspectives are shaded, and the buildings stand on rudimentarily depicted sites. They are in presentation only halfway between Shaw's views and those of Downing.[29]

Just as Shaw's *Rural Architecture* failed to keep up in design and presentation with the contemporary publications of Downing, Davis, and others, so comparison of his *The Modern Architect* of 1854 to Samuel Sloan's two-volume *The Model Architect* of 1852, published in Philadelphia, shows that the Boston author's approach, dating back to his eleven-year-old *Rural Architecture*, had become woefully out of step with the times. Sloan's is the work of an architect a full generation younger than Shaw. It is a handsome catalogue of knowledgeable designs in the Italianate, Elizabethan, Gothic, Norman, and other newly introduced historic styles presented in plan and details, but especially in rendered elevations showing the building in the landscape, and in perspectives of the kind Shaw had called for two decades earlier in *Civil Architecture*, but had never himself delivered. The Bostonian's early title continued to appear in reprints through the rest of the century, perhaps because its lack of model designs kept it from looking so old fashioned and its practical text remained useful.

Because architecture and its history were subjects of interest among the educated of Boston more generally then than now, Shaw might also have had useful access to the private libraries of laymen whom he knew. The realization of his publications and their intellectual presentation owed something to his reference to works outside the field of architecture. For example, in the Introduction to the second edition of *Civil Architecture*, dated May 1832, a brief history of architecture as well as other subjects, Shaw cites the Bible; T. B. Armstrong's *Journal of Travels in the Seat of War* (1831); and Theodore Dwight's, *A Journal of a Tour in Italy in the Year 1821* (1821). He also mentions Diodorus Siculus, whose *Bibliotheca historica* was available in English by 1814 (although it is likely that Shaw found him in a secondary source, as might have been true, as we said, of many of his references). Nonarchitectural authors mentioned in *Rural Architecture* are William Bullock, probably his *Six Months' Residence and Travels in Mexico* (1824), and Vivant Denon, *Travels in Upper and Lower Egypt* (1802). His remarks on Jeremy Bentham here are taken word for word from Hewson Clarke's *Cabinet of Arts* (1817). The lists suggest that Shaw was a first- or second-hand reader of what was then popular literature. We find nothing like the degree of these citations in the works of his competitors.

Shaw may have been introduced to such reading by acquaintances outside his workplace. He acknowledges the suggestions and additions of Charles W. Moore to his Introduction and text of the second edition (1832) of *Civil Architecture*. This suggests that Moore, a seasoned historian and writer, helped Shaw revise his first effort at publication. And this could have been at the behest of one of the enlightened partners of Shaw's new publishing house, Marsh, Capen & Lyon. Charles Whitlock Moore (1801–73) was a printer, publisher, editor, author, and major figure in the Masonic world in and beyond Boston. Among Moore's many publications, germane here was the *Boston Masonic Mirror* (of which he was editor and which appeared under the name of Moore & [Edwin] Sevey) from 1830 to 1834. Spread over the issues for April and May 1831 of that journal is a long, detailed, unsigned review of the first edition of *Civil Architecture*. Most likely written by Moore himself, it is by far the most complete notice of the work to appear. (It is worth noticing that Moore did not review any of Benjamin's titles that appeared in those years.) The review is descriptive rather than critical. Having perused Shaw's first edition Moore may have suggested some revisions and additions to the second.

In the middle 1830s Moore briefly joined William W. Wheildon's *Bunker Hill Aurora* (1834–65), with the two men co-editing the result and both living in Charlestown.[30] Wheildon, a well-remembered author of many works on local history, was then at the beginning of a long career as distinguished editor of the *Aurora*. He too was a Mason, but the man's interest went well beyond that affiliation. Wheildon's *Memoir of Solomon Willard* of 1865, for example, is the standard source for the biography of one of Shaw's major architectural contemporaries. In the late 1820s, Moore was involved with the formation of the Boston Mechanics' Institution (not to be confused with the older Massachusetts Charitable Mechanic Association[31]), which was intended to include "mechanics and others as are friendly to the promotion of Science and the Arts." Its object was "the cultivation of useful knowledge, by the aid of lectures," and other means. The distinguished mathematician Nathaniel Bowditch was President; Solomon Willard a Vice-President. Charles W. Moore sat among the founding directors, as did Alexander Parris.[32] And it may have been through Moore that Shaw met one of his earliest clients, for, as we shall see, William Wheildon commissioned two townhouses from the architect in 1830, or about the time *Civil Architecture* began to reach completion. Of course, it is also possible that Moore introduced Wheildon to his architect.

We have nothing at this point to indicate that Shaw was ever active in the Mechanics' Institution, but Charles W. Moore was not his only acquaintance who was. In *Rural Architecture* Shaw quotes a letter from the Rev. John Pierpont, which says that "in compliance with your request" Pierpont sends "the dimensions of the different parts of the columns of that most exquisite of all the specimens of the Doric architecture,—the Parthenon,—from my own careful measurement, in April, 1836." John Pierpont (1785–1866) was a characteristic nineteenth-century Boston activist-intellectual: a Unitarian clergyman; lecturer; author; poet; advocate of phrenology, spiritualism, and temperance; among other things. And he was briefly a director of the Boston Mechanics' Institution in the early 1830s. His tenure at the Hollis Street Church lasted from 1819 to 1845, during which he traveled to Europe and the East. That Shaw requested such accurate information seems to indicate that he was a serious scholar who, when possible, went to the source for information. Like his colleagues, he was determined to copy correctly the details of classical design.

According to contemporary newspaper accounts, in December 1835 Pierpont was in Rome, and in June, Smyrna. It is doubtful that he would have skipped Athens then. He must have taken his measurements on that trip, as the date of his letter stipulates. When he sent his results to Shaw is unknown, but Shaw published them in his *Rural Architecture* as dated June 10, 1843, and republished them in *The Modern Architect* as dated June 10, 1853. Was Shaw, or were his publishers, trying to make his sources appear to be up to date?

In a reminiscence published in the *Boston Transcript* for January 5, 1903, the architect Thomas W. Silloway asserted that "Shaw's Civil Architecture" was "written mainly—as Mr. Shaw once informed me [some fifty years earlier]—by the late Rev. John Pierpont, at the time minister of the Hollis Street Church." But Pierpont's name does not appear in any edition of that early title. In the section on the Doric order in *Rural Architecture* (and again in *The Modern Architect*) he does appear. It was Moore whom Shaw credits with help in the second edition of *Civil Architecture*. It may be that the elder Silloway confused Pierpont with Moore.

Other names should be mentioned among Shaw's important Boston connections. One is that of the Rev. Louis Dwight, whom we know collaborated or consulted with the architect on a couple of projects in the 1830s. As head of the Boston Prison Discipline Society from 1826, Dwight was a "promoter of prison betterment, a missionary in heart, and an impassioned fighter for what he believed to be right."[33] He spearheaded the prison reform movement and became an authority on the architecture of incarceration. In the competition for The Tombs in New York City, the entry by Dwight and Shaw won third prize. Dwight also collaborated with other architects such as Gridley J. F. Bryant.[34] Both Dwight and Bryant appear in the list of buildings mentioned below in competition with Shaw for the Deer Island Almshouse Hospital. Dwight's prescription for a "good prison" appeared in 1846 in the twenty-first annual report of the Prison Discipline Society.

In addition to his collaboration with Dwight, and an occasional association with his fellow architects, such as William Sparrell, Shaw seems to have had some connection from time to time with the noted civil engineer, landscape architect, and busy surveyor, Alexander Wadsworth, a cousin of the poet.[35] At his death it was said that Wadsworth had drawn "many thousands of plans, as he surveyed a large part of the city and its suburbs." Wadsworth laid out cemeteries, including, with Henry A. S. Dearborn, Mount Auburn in Cambridge, as well as parks and suburban developments, such as Webster Park in West Newton, for which Shaw appears to have provided a design for ten Gothic houses. Wadsworth also surveyed many individual residential lots, including that for Shaw's Thaxter house on Mount Vernon Street. The relationship between the two men was not necessarily close, for Wadsworth seems to have worked for "everybody" in his long, productive life.

More detailed information about Edward Shaw's biography and his Boston contemporary connections would be most welcome, especially some explanation of the process by which the carpenter became an author. We have enough to assert that he was well versed in the sources of information for both the practical and theoretical aspects of the professional status to which he helped others to aspire through his books; that through his own skills, the literary sources at his disposal by whatever means, and his social connections within the profession and without, he rose to a significant position in the architectural life of Boston during his maturity; and, through his books, produced a body of professional literature to challenge that of his generation and spread his name across the country. Although of his built legacy little survives, for the many editions and reprints of his books alone he deserves a position among the better known of his antebellum Boston contemporaries. But a detailed understanding of the process by which he decided to set down his hammer, at least figuratively, and take up the pen, awaits further documentation.

2

BUILDINGS

The list of known Shaw-designed projects is short, and that of his buildings that survive even shorter. Largely because of the existence of several portfolios of his drawings, we know almost as much about the projects he did not build as the few we know he did. When he briefly outlined his career in the footnote to the advertisement in *The Modern Architect,* as we have seen, Shaw wrote that in his early years as a contractor he had drawn all of his "own plans and designs for private and public dwellings." What they looked like we do not know. His development as a draftsman is lost. Of the seven sets of drawings that we now know have survived, the earliest dates from 1832 (contemporary with the second edition of *Civil Architecture* and the only edition of *Operative Masonry*), when he was forty-eight years old, and the remainder produced during, approximately, the years he spent his time "in the theoretical practice and science of Architectural Drawings and Plans." What we have are mature graphics and they are, in general, much like those of his contemporaries. Shaw usually bound them into portfolios, provided a title page, worked on more or less legal-size wove sheets for domestic designs and larger sheets for more important buildings, used ink and gray or colored washes, and employed "backlining"—the emphasizing of some lines to give life to a black-and-white orthogonal drawing—and rare cast shadows inconsistently.[36] Although he advocates the creation of rendered perspectives of proposed buildings set into indications of landscaping for the instruction of clients in his *Civil Architecture,* no known drawing from his hand meets his own requirement.

Shaw seems to have been the darling of the city's press, who were wont to praise his skill at planning, but he lacked the patronage of city or county headquarters or the State House that would have assured him important civil commissions. We know of only one executed public work for the Boston area, the austere Middlesex County House of Correction (now gone), and another for the Manchester Town House in his native New Hampshire. His books focus primarily on domestic design with a minor role given over to ecclesiastical works and a couple of shopfronts. Nonetheless, we know something about his approach to larger commissions from a number of surviving competition drawings. And his list of clients, however short, was an impressive one, including Boston's wealthiest citizens, men like David Sears II and George Parkman, and some important businessmen such as Adam W. Thaxter, Jr. and Deming Jarvis. That learned gentlemen, such as the Rev. John Pierpont and Charles W. Moore, contributed to his books also suggests that his circle of private supporters was an elevated one.

His faintly Gothic houses in West Newton seem to have been based on his drawing for a private commission now preserved at Historic New England. The houses survive, but they have been altered and are of less interest than his three other surviving works: the standard façade of a Beacon Hill townhouse on Pinkney Street of 1833, the Thaxter House of 1836–37 on Mt. Vernon Street, also on the

Hill, and the aforementioned Town House (now part of City Hall) of 1844–45 in Manchester. The latter two represent the loci of his life and embrace with distinction the poles of popular architectural style of the late 1820s to the 1840s. The Thaxter House has a frontispiece that is universally admired by aficionados as a textbook example of Grecian Revival design; the Town Hall is among the more inventive works of the early Gothic Revival in this country. Other of Shaw's projects are known in some detail from his portfolios of drawings, as noted above, and others in lesser detail from newspapers and other contemporary sources. His surviving buildings in Boston and Manchester show him capable of first-class work, but from what we learn based on the evidence of his drawings, it is apparent that Shaw's buildings did not rank with the Granite Style works of the most distinguished of his contemporaries. Were it not for his publications, he would probably have remained as little known as colleagues such as Joseph Jenkins or Cornelius Coolidge.

SOME MINOR EARLY WORKS

Wales's Tavern, Newton Lower Falls, 1832

On July 5, 1832, Nathaniel Wales of Newton, inn holder, and Daniel Kingsbury, Jr. of Newton, carpenter, signed a contract engaging Kingsbury to build by November 30 of that year a framed "house designed for a hotel or public house" at Lower Falls, to conform to the plan and specifications of Edward Shaw, Architect.[37] Little else has come to light about this commission. An image by William Hollis of what is said to be Wales's Tavern, with an inaccurate caption, appears in a recent book on Newton.[38] The sketch, said to date from 1864, shows a presumably four-story frame structure consisting of a one-story piazza surrounding a two-story block above which two more floors step back to produce a pyramidal overall profile. The building, which sat on the verge of the Charles River, served as a stage stop until destroyed by fire in 1868.[39]

American Amphitheatre, Boston, 1832

Also in 1832, William Pelby, actor and theater manager, set up his own establishment to rival the Tremont Theatre on Tremont Street. He acquired for his purposes the equestrian amphitheater at Portland and Traverse streets in Boston. To quote Richard Foster Stoddard,[40] "called the American Amphitheatre, this structure had been erected at a cost of only $1100 by Jeremiah, Theodore, and William Washburn, contractors, following a design by Edward Shaw." (The same year, the Washburns endorsed the first edition of Shaw's *Civil Architecture*.) The Amphitheatre opened in February 1832. When Pelby bought the building he agreed to allow equestrian performances during three months of the year. But he was soon making extensive alterations to turn it into a theater, including the substitution of a pit for an equestrian ring. He opened the building as the Warren Theatre. It is under that name that it appears in a sketch in Bowen's *Picture of Boston*.[41] It is difficult to say how much of what we see in the little drawing was due to Shaw. It looks to have been a central rotunda with a cupola (for vents?) embraced by corner building blocks. Such a circular form would have been well suited to equestrian displays, but with one section open, for a theater audience as well.

DOMESTIC ARCHITECTURE

Row and Other Houses, 1820s to 1840s

Shaw found work as a designer and supervisor of construction for row houses standing along the streets of greater Boston. Like many of his peers, men like Isaiah Rogers, William Sparrill, Richard Bond, Charles Roath, and John Kutts, with these jobs he had a repetitive source of income trying to keep up with the housing demands of a burgeoning city. Between 1820 and 1850 the population of Boston rose from 43,000 to 136,000 while its land mass expanded as well. Between 1827 and 1846, Shaw laid out well over forty city dwellings. The list is known from the files of the Suffolk County Registry of Deeds, where building contracts were recorded.[42] It could not have been inspiring work, for possible variations in plan, façade, details, or materials were minimal. It did, however, pay the bills and place the architect's name before the public. Only very rarely do the drawings for this kind of commission survive, because they are often used up in the process. With one outstanding exception, the extraordinary Thaxter House, Shaw's drawings for urban domestic work as well as many of the houses themselves would appear to have vanished, the latter in the churning physical history of the Hub.

Based on surviving records, Shaw's clients were mainly builders, such as masons and carpenters, or speculators who ordered several attached houses at once. Three names of other types of clients stand out: in 1830 the twenty-five-year-old future editor and historian, William W. Wheildon, had Shaw design two narrow brick houses on Back Street in Charleston, one surely for himself (and perhaps the other for Charles W. Moore). The next year brought a commission from Deming Jarvis, recent founder of the well-known Boston and Ipswich Glass Company, for a house at 71 Summer Street.[43] In 1835 the distinguished physician George Parkman asked for a brick row house in Berry Street. Parkman was the scion of one of Boston's wealthiest families, a man often seen in the city's streets collecting his rents, whose gruesome murder by Harvard professor John White Webster fourteen years later shocked the city.[44] The Shaw-designed house was surely a rental property, for Parkman lived on Beacon Hill. The complex financial details of the doctor's contract with Samuel Decoster, housewright, defy understanding by anyone but, perhaps, an astute accountant with an interest in real estate history.

Surviving contracts for these commissions, which probably represent only part of Shaw's urban domestic catalogue, provide a wealth of detail (and nomenclature) about the domestic architectural scene in Boston in the first half of the nineteenth century. Shaw provided guidance for domestic building in his several books, but the contracts also offer detailed descriptions of construction, thus providing a substitute for specifications when none were attached. Lot widths ranged from twenty-two to some thirty feet (Wheildon's in Charlestown was a mere seventeen feet wide). Most townhouses had a lighted cellar, raised main floor reached by exterior steps, front and back parlors divided by sliding doors, a side hall with stairs, a chamber or bedroom floor, and one or two floors above reached by the stairway lit from a skylight. The attic would be lighted by one or more "lutherans" or dormers. The triangular section beneath the ridgepole and above the attic was known as a "cockloft." Depending on location, chimneypieces might be marble or soapstone or wood. Façades were of brick with, perhaps, stone trim; storefronts might be of Concord or Chelmsford stone or Quincy granite. Receiving potable and discharging waste water was a major concern, especially prior to the opening of the fresh-water aqueduct from Cochituate in 1848. Such houses were erected as standard dwellings for the middle class. The townhouse Shaw designed for Thaxter in Mount Vernon Street on Beacon Hill was, of course, custom designed and intended for a more affluent merchant, but the interior arrangement of rooms was similar to the average house.

For the earliest townhouse to come to light, commissioned by lumber merchant George I. Galvin, Shaw designed in 1827 two brick dwellings at the corner of Dedham Turnpike and Cottage Street in Roxbury, as well as two houses in Essex Street in Boston, to be erected by David Cobbett and Edward Maxwell, masons, and Abraham M. Green and Edward Hatch, housewrights, "agreeable to a plan . . . by Edward Shaw." Galvin returned to Shaw, and one Peter Johnson, briefly Shaw's associate and otherwise unknown, for two houses on Pearl Street in Boston in 1828, and the same year to Shaw alone for six more houses on the same street. Meanwhile the architect laid out two houses in Winter Street for Isaac Towle, housewright, and Slade Luther (whom we shall meet again) and David Nichols, bricklayers, and he and William Sparrell joined forces to design two dwellings in Washington Street for a housewright, a mason, and a lawyer. It was to have features "like those in Charles Haywards's house in Hayward Place," perhaps another Shaw or Shaw and Sparrell design. Hayward was a justice of the peace. In 1824 he advertised two new furnished houses in Hayward Square for rent. Obviously all this action was pure speculation. The façades of some of these row houses were varied by the incorporation of ground-floor storefronts. For merchant Isaac Davis, Shaw drafted three such hybrid buildings in Hanover Street in the North End in 1829, buildings according to the contract that were to "most strictly conform to the plans drawn by E. Shaw."[45]

The year 1832 brought a building for merchant Charles Blanchard, perhaps in Roxbury. The year 1834 produced commissions from several clients: a house in Stoddard Street for John B. Hammett, an upholsterer, another for him on the corner of Howard and Stoddard, and a commercial stable for Newell Towle in Charles Street. Shaw laid out a frame house in South Boston for Michael Burns that was not deemed acceptable until the construction was approved by the architect. He drafted a plan for a house in Temple Street for Asahel Gilbert, a carpenter, in 1837; and in the same year two Boston tenements for Henry Dawes, broker, to follow the "plan and annexed specifications drawn by Edward Shaw." Then came four houses in Southac Street for William Foster, mason, in 1838; a three-story brick house in Endicott Street for Charles Bowen in 1840; a dwelling with piazza and stable for town clerk and later magistrate, Artemas Newell of Brookline, in 1842 "in conformity with a plan and specifications . . . drawn by Edward Shaw"; two "brick and slated" houses for builder Ferdinand G. Simpson in Marion Street in 1843; three two-and-one-half-story, wooden houses with finished attics in May Street for John Smith, laborer, and Elijah Smith, mariner, in 1845. They were to be habitable in four months. In April of the next year, Edward A. Raymond sold the site upon which Isaiah Rogers's Howard Athenaeum would be erected and commissioned nine brick slate-roofed houses in the Waltham Street area of South Boston to be built "according in all respects to the specifications and plans prepared by Edward Shaw." It should be noted that all of this work occurred in the years Shaw was issuing or reissuing the first of his books.

Row House, 4 Pinkney Street, Boston, 1832–33

On February 21, 1833, Francis L. Bates and Nathaniel B. Frost, masons, hired George Spinney, housewright, to do the carpentry work in the "unfinished three story brick house situated in Pinkney Street." The work was to be performed "according to a plan . . . drawn by Edward Shaw," and the workers were to examine features of "Mr. [James] Picken's house in [42] Bowdoin Street," perhaps another Shaw design.[46] Bates and Frost took out a mortgage on the property on June 27, 1833. It was apparently used as a rental property until midcentury.

The three-bay, three-story brick and stone-trimmed façade fronts one of the two known surviving Beacon Hill houses certainly designed by Shaw. The crisp, flat, severely rectangular grid of frameless window openings is relieved by the entrance, with its framed side and overhead glazing. It is a close cousin to those "Designs for Out-Side Doors" Shaw published in Plate 72 of his contemporary *Civil Architecture.*

Adam Wallace Thaxter, Jr. House, Boston, 1836–37

Rising (literally) above the bulk of Shaw's other urban domestic works is the house designed for businessman Adam Wallace Thaxter, Jr. in 1836–37. It stands at 59 Mount Vernon Street on Beacon Hill, completely at home in that architecturally impressive location. Although some changes have been made by later owners, who included the editor, novelist, and poet Thomas Bailey Aldrich, much of the original layout and many details survive.[47]

Thaxter was a principal in the Commercial Wharf establishment of Bates & Co., a concern that traded chiefly with Holland and Russia. "No firm in Boston stood higher as merchants."[48] He was also to hold the post of vice-president of the Boston Five Cent Savings Bank incorporated in 1854.[49] Except for his Democratic politics (he stood without success for several local offices), he was the perfect model of a well-fixed, patriotic Bostonian of his time who, among other signs of his class, hung Copley's portrait of Samuel Adams among other such icons in his new house, and in 1853 served on the building committee for Gridley J. F. Bryant's addition to the State House, just a few steps up the street.[50] Also representative of his class is the preservation of a rare cache of original documents about the house, including Shaw's drawings and specifications, his charges, builders' contracts, and drawings for later changes to the house proposed by Bryant.[51]

A survey survives of the building lot drawn by busy Alexander Wadsworth dated March 11, 1836. Shaw's (apparently preliminary) drawings, scaled at one inch to eight feet but not dimensioned, for which he received $75 on November 15 of the same year according to an invoice drawn up on the last day of 1837, include plans of the cellar, the "basement" (that is, the slightly raised first or entry floor), the "parlour" floor, and the attic. What would have been the plan of the chamber or bedroom floor above the parlors is either missing or never drawn (that floor was also omitted from the printed specifications and its dimensions had to be added freehand). Walls of all the plans are pochéd (in red) and backlined.

There is nothing distinctive about the overall interior layout; there is in its execution (Fig. 2). The entry to the right of the south-facing street façade leads into the hall with its impressive stairway of swirling steps and handrails that flow into raking scrolls. An enclosed service stair lies beyond. To the left of the entrance is a pair of connected rooms. The bow, or "swell" (as such a feature was then usually called) of the façade shapes one wall of the front room, and that is echoed by another, concave interior wall, beyond which are a pair of closets. The north room (the dining room) is rectangular. A fireplace is centered on the west wall of each, as they were intended to be where possible on the floors above, as we know from one of the longitudinal sections.

The hall stair spins up from the entry level to the floor above where it lands across from a pair of parlors separated by a sliding door. The room toward the

Plan of Basement Floor

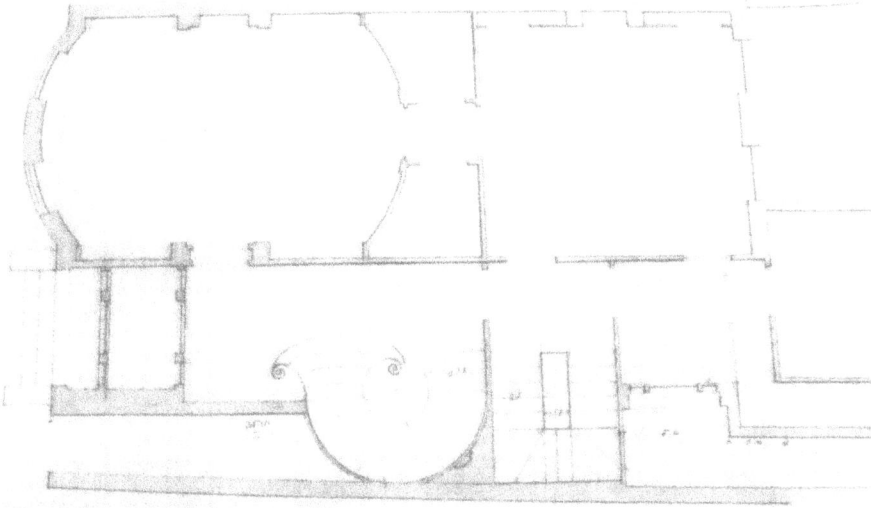

Figure 2 Edward Shaw, *Plan of the Parlour Floor,* Adam W. Thaxter, Jr. House, Mt. Vernon Street, Beacon Hill, Boston, 1836–37. Courtesy of Special Collections, Fine Arts Library, Harvard University.

street is shaped by the swell; that to the rear is a rectangle. The circular stair continues beneath its skylight through the chamber floor to the attic with its four corner rooms beneath the roof. Lutherans are indicated front and rear. A straight stair leads up to the observatory indicated only on the drawing for the façade. Another sheet shows an ell attached to the east of the main block containing kitchen, washroom, and a many-holed privy.

There are two longitudinal sections: one through the staircase, the other through the rooms. The former is a preliminary, not a definitive, drawing, and would appear to precede the latter. Both show the chamber floor. The main stair is not yet defined; it begins from the entrance hall as a straight flight, then curves up to the attic floor. The adjacent service stair is shown ending at the chamber floor. The story above would have been used by the servants, who could reach it via the top flight of the main stair; the Thaxters would presumably never climb that except when visiting the observatory. Above the attic is a cockloft with stair rising into the observatory. The section through the rooms shows chimneypieces, paneled doors, and the Ionic pilasters of the front room on the entry level. They are detailed in an elevation of the room showing the wall treatment. The doorway between rooms is framed with fluted pilasters supporting a low pediment above an architrave decorated with rosettes. The wall pilasters "support" low pediments

Figure 3   Edward Shaw, main stair, Thaxter House, Boston. Photo ca. 1900. Courtesy of Historic New England.

set against an architrave also carrying rosettes. Much of this original ornament remains in the house; some has been recreated.[52]

The most dramatic feature of the interior is the circular stairway rising from the entry hall (Fig. 3). In his *Rural Architecture* (1843), Shaw describes such a staircase as admitting, if large, "greater beauty" than a rectangular one and, if small, "greater conveniency" [*sic*]. Certainly both are true in a narrow townhouse.

He goes on to say that when there is room, "it is usual to put on a curtail step and scroll-rail, supported with an iron newel, and up the rail are several iron balusters to secure the same." As we shall see, his specifications here detail such an arrangement.

The existing Mt. Vernon street façade conforms to the elevation drawn by Shaw (Fig. 4). The two ground-floor windows in the swell to the left are tall, six-over-nine light rectangles with low pediments for caps as shown at larger scale on a separate drawing. The four windows on each of the two floors above are six-over-six lights caped with lintels. Blinds are not shown. The cornice atop the wall is decorated with leafy wreaths, one for each window. The four lutherans on the roof are smaller eight-over-eight lights. A simple iron fence runs between the embracing chimneys and the crenelated walls of the octagonal observatory. A conical skylight over the circular stairway appears to the right. The drafted elevation also depicts the much-admired Grecian, distyle-in-antis frontispiece above a short flight of steps. Another drawing at larger scale details that entryway with its low-sloped pediment (Fig. 5). Shaw listed on his itemized invoice "2 days work on Plan for Frontispiece" on January 18, 1837. In May, John Templeman billed Thaxter $93 for "Cutting 2 Ornamental Caps" for the exterior of the windows at this level, and "Flutting Colloms" on the frontispiece (Fig. 6). A note on this bill over Shaw's signature suggests that the amounts Templeman charged for his work exceeded the agreed upon prices.

The contract for masonry work was signed by Thaxter and Thomas Moulton, brick layer, on March 6, 1837, with October 1 specified as the date on which the house was to be ready for occupancy. The agreement called for payment in stages to Moulton of $9,770. A second contract signed the same day engaged carpenters Luther Farwell and Elisha Magoun to work on the same schedule for $7,000. Both contracts were accompanied by printed specifications "drawn by Edward Shaw, Architect."[53] A few excerpts: both gave the width as 31 feet in front and 32 in the rear, and 45 feet deep (no mention of the service ell). Vertical dimensions are given as 8 feet cellar, 11 feet 6 inches entry floor, 12 feet parlor floor, 10 feet chambers (this added in ink; as noted above, this floor was overlooked in the set of plans[54]), and 8 feet attic. Such shifting ceiling heights were commonly specified at the time. In *Rural Architecture*, Shaw says that for reasons of health no ceiling should be less than ten feet, but that apparently did not apply to servants' rooms in the attic.

Quincy granite "under pining" is called for in the specifications, with the front façade "laid up as per plan with the first quality of face or pressed brick" bound with "tile" every fifth course. The roof to be of "the best quality of 'ladies slate,' with sawed butts fastened with copper nails." In the slating section of *Civil Architecture*, Shaw describes the specified roofing as from Wales, and similar to slate from Scotland that is in "little repute. . . . They are fragments of larger

Figure 4 Edward Shaw, *Front Elevation*, Thaxter House, Boston. Courtesy of Special Collections, Fine Arts Library, Harvard University.

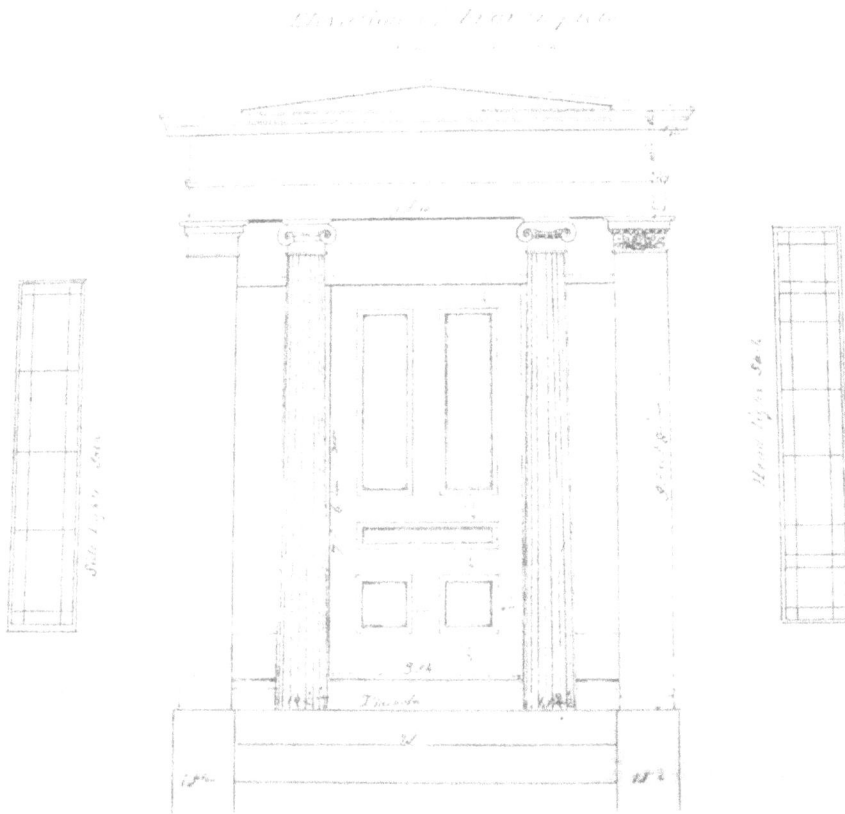

Figure 5 Edward Shaw, *Elevation of Frontispiece*, Thaxter House, Boston. Courtesy of Special Collections, Fine Arts Library, Harvard University.

slates." He sizes them as 1' 3" x 8" and describes the method of laying them. His specifications go on to say that the "cupola" was to be covered with sheet lead, and the "circular part in front of Lutheran windows [was] to be covered with copper."

Interior walls and ceilings were to be furred and plastered. Basement and parlor rooms "to have stucco cornices and entablatures; also stucco centre pieces in the front entry . . . of such pattern as the owner shall choose." This organization is shown in a large elevation of an interior wall of the entry level, as noted above (Fig. 7). Where there have been changes in the interior of the rooms, including later chimneypieces, reference to both Shaw's section through the rooms and Plates 73–74 of the fourth (1836) edition of his *Civil Architecture* will suggest the original design. Doors with "pannels" are specified for every doorway. The front door was to be made of black walnut, basement and parlor doors of bay mahogany, panels veneered with branch mahogany, all varnished. Cherry sashes for all windows, except those in the attic. Cherry or mahogany bannisters for the

Figure 6   Frontispiece, Thaxter House, Boston. Courtesy Earle G. Shettleworth, Jr.

front flight of stairs, with "a proper number of iron bannisters to support the [mahogany] rail." These woods seem to have been a common mix of the time.

   Producing the original design was far from the end of Shaw's commitment to the house. The invoice of his charges through 1837 shows that he revised his plans until the March signing of contracts and then, beginning in early April, visited the site on 110 days until early December. He billed Thaxter $772.75 for drawing and supervising. The standing house, despite various alterations over time, shows that construction followed closely Shaw's drawings. Other documents

Figure 7   Edward Shaw, *Style of Basement Room Finish*, Thaxter House, Boston. Courtesy of Special Collections, Fine Arts Library, Harvard University.

indicate that Thaxter kept a close eye on all expenses. Leonard Holton billed the owner $1250 for 25,000 bricks carted up from Beacon Street. Among many others that are notable is a proposal in June from John Fleming that lists chimneypieces of various sizes: two large Egyptian marble chimneypieces, two "Dove color," three Egyptian marble, and six white marble. A bill of October from Fleming for 14 "Marble Chimney Pieces with Hearths" of various sizes came to $594. This is endorsed by Shaw "if the prices agree with with [*sic*] your engagement [with] Mr Fleming."

The completion of the house seems to have been ragged. Thaxter had to call in a pair of referees—Slade Luther, a wealthy mason, and John Clark, perhaps the commercial merchant listed in city directories—to settle a dispute with Moulton. He then supplied them with a list of problems (he called them "objections") that needed to be solved but for which he had been billed. The referees, "having given a full hearing of the Parties and a thorough examination of the Case," allowed some of Moulton's charges in December, but in June of the next year, although he had "hoped to avoid troubling you [the referees] further regarding my a/c with Mr. Moulton," Thaxter did just that. Although it is difficult at this distance to understand the documentation in detail, it is clear that construction ended, as many others did and still do, with owner and builder jockeying to put paid to the process.

31

Among the existing papers related to the Thaxter House is a second survey
of the property by Alexander Wadsworth, dated April 24, 1852, that is actually
a copy by Gridley J. F. Bryant. It shows the house only in outline, including the
bow that then existed in the north wall of the rear room of the entry floor. Bryant
must have agreed to remodel the residence while he and Thaxter were concerned
with the State House. A plan, dated April 21st shows the rear section of the
house with its service wing "as it now is." A swell is shown bulging out from
the dining room on the entry level. It is largely glazed and extended by a low
balcony overlooking the rear garden. Except for that feature, which does not show
up on Shaw's earliest plans, the ell is laid out reasonably close to what he drew.
It has been updated probably several times in the history of the house. What
are presumably drawings from Bryant's office dated April–May for "proposed"
changes include the cellar, "First" or entry level, and "Second" or parlor level.
Nothing in the drawings for this proposed alteration is of much interest regarding
Shaw, except that they show the dining room swell. As the swell appears on
Wadsworth's survey, prepared before Bryant's drawings, it seems that it could
have been among the changes Shaw drew in early 1837. But without further
evidence, that must remain speculation.[55]

With the exception of its frontispiece, the Thaxter House is a splendid example
of the conservative contemporary residences of Beacon Hill, characterized by
Talbot Hamlin as "of red brick, with large ample windows, occasional iron
balconies, and delicate cornices and doorways."[56] Stylistically, it is precisely
what an architect of Shaw's generation would produce: a hybrid of the Federal
and the Greek. Its rare Grecian frontispiece, however, is often remembered as
an outstanding detail of Beacon Hill architecture. A photograph of it appeared
in Howard Major's pioneering *The Domestic Architecture of the Early American
Republic* of 1926 as a textbook example of the Grecian revival.

William W. Warren ("West India") House, Arlington, 1840

The Warren House stood in West Chester, now Arlington, Massachusetts, on the
western shore of Spy Pond. Altered with a mansard roof and other changes in
the 1870s for Samuel D. Hicks, a Boston coppersmith, it burned to the ground
in 1934.[57] William Wilkins Warren had been an "eminent merchant" on St.
Thomas in the Virgin Islands in the 1830s.[58] He returned to the mainland in
1840. In his autobiography of 1884, Warren noted that he purchased the five-
acre West Chester lot from his brother-in-law, William Schouler, then an editor
and politician. "This [presumably the lot] was laid out on a plan I had drawn
while at sea," wrote Warren; "a Doric villa was erected and hundreds of trees
and shrubs set out the same year. . . . The place was much admired, and from
its novel construction was called the West India House." He sold the property
in 1846.[59]

Surviving drawings consist of a bound set of four elevations as well as two plans in ink and watercolor on wove paper, all of the former signed by Shaw, now in the collection of Historic New England. A note on the verso of the fifth sheet reads: "Wm. W. Warren's Plans of / house to be built by / Adam S. Cottrell as per / contract signed this day / July 30, 1840." The drawings are certainly by Shaw, but the design must represent a more than usual collaboration between client and architect. Its West Indies aura surely reflected Warren's recollection of buildings he had left behind in the Caribbean. The house is unique in Shaw's known oeuvre, as indeed it was in contemporary Boston architecture.

Although long gone, a precise understanding of the Warren house and grounds can be retrieved from the drawings, including landscape plans, and the description published at the time of the sale in 1846. According to the latter, the site contained "a beautiful grove of forest trees on the banks of the pond, about 140 thriving young fruit trees, of the choicest varieties, upwards of 200 young forest trees, besides grape and raspberry vines, fruit and flowering shrubs, &c., and a kitchen and flower garden." The unsigned landscape plans that survive are labeled in script that closely resembles that of Edward Shaw on signed drawings for the house[60] (Fig. 8). These might be the architect's redraft of Warren's idea for his property "drawn while at sea." They are unusual in the site planning of the time. The house is set within a closed circular drive tangent on axis with a half-circular approach from the main road. The barn sits farther back along the same axis, the vegetable garden beyond that. Fruit trees are noted to either side in areas reached by three-sided gates placed on the cross-axis of the plan. The pattern of drives on the property shown on a real estate map made of the area after the Hicks purchase suggests that this layout was followed on the ground.

When the house went on the market in 1846 it was said to have been built "in the most thorough manner, with slated roof and cupola, . . . two wings connected in the rear, and joining the main building, . . . which has also a spacious piazza on three sides." The basement story contained "kitchen, store [room], wash rooms, dining-room, bedroom, and large cellar." The upper floor held three parlors, four [bed] chambers, "and a large bathing room." The attic, not shown on the surviving set of drawings, contained "spacious sleeping rooms." A Bryant and Hermann furnace supplied heat;[61] water arrived by way of a "forced pump from an excellent well and cistern." The whole had been "completed . . . according to plans by, and under the superintendence of one of the best architects of this city." The plans of the house show an axial layout conforming to the axial arrangement of the landscape, with axial stairs rising from the ground to the piazza, an axial corridor leading through the "main building" with its parlor, sitting room, and two chambers, into an entry corridor, across an entry piazza, and down steps into the enclosed yard. The "main building" forms the fat stem of a T-shaped plan whose crossbar, set on the cross axis of the grounds, contained a chamber and adjoining bedroom and another chamber with adjoining bathroom.

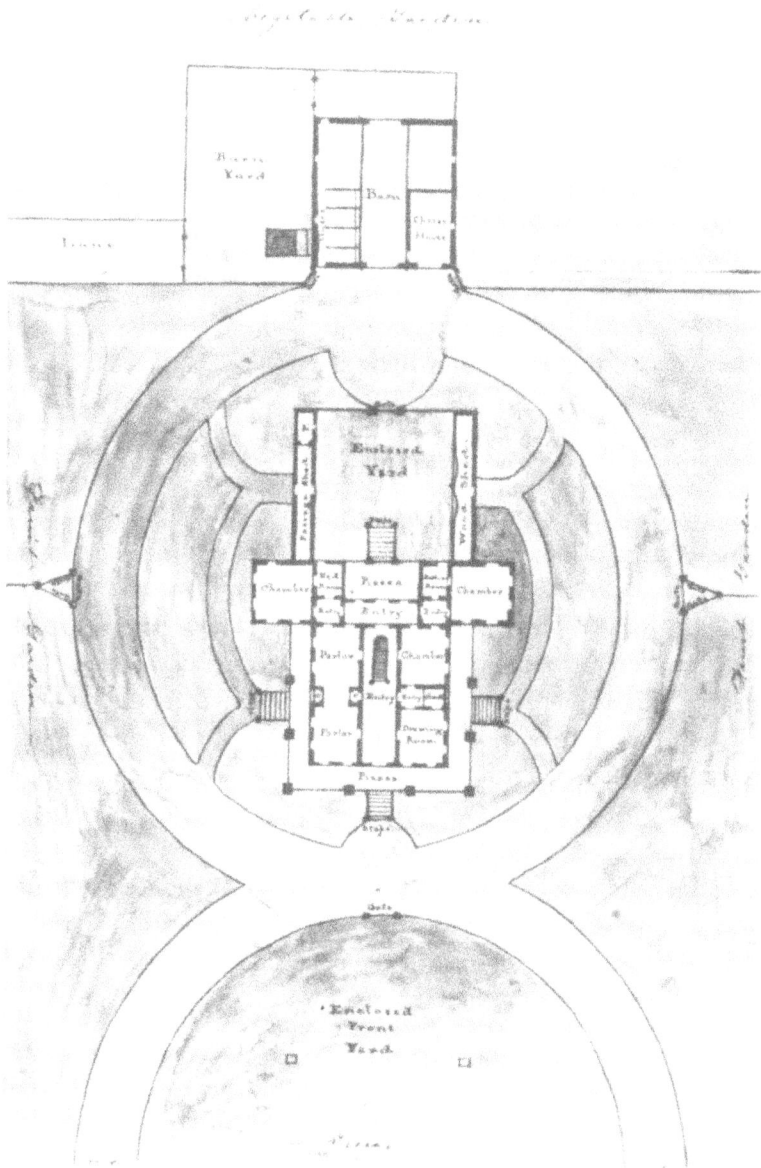

Figure 8 Attributed to Edward Shaw, Estate plan for the William W. Warren House, Arlington, Massachusetts, 1840. Courtesy Historic New England.

The drafted elevations, shown standing on rudimentary suggestions of site, detail a three-sided piazza with Doric columns sustaining a low gable roof whose ridge follows the main axis of the entire layout (Fig. 9). It is surmounted by a square cupola. In keeping with the Doric order, all details are plain. The rear elevation shows the outlines of two shed-like structures right and left of the axis. These are explained by reference to the landscape drawings, where they are

Figure 9 Edward Shaw, *Front Elevation*, Warren House, Arlington. Courtesy Historic New England.

labeled on one side "Passage Shed" leading to a room called "P.," surely a privy, and on the other "Wood Shed." These delineate two sides of the enclosed rear yard. The third side is fenced, with an axial gate leading to the barn. In Shaw's design, architecture and landscape combined to produce an original domestic setting for the Boston area in the 1840s. The originality stemmed from the joining of an imaginative client and a responsive architect.

David Sears II House, Brookline, 1842–43

David Sears II, scion of one of the richest families in Boston, who in 1842 was the city's wealthiest resident, acquired 200 acres in Brookline and proceeded to develop it, with the assistance of Alexander Wadsworth, into the garden suburb called Longwood.[62] For his own use there he commissioned a house from Edward Shaw, thus becoming the architect's most well-heeled client. At the time, Sears was living in Beacon Street in a landmark house designed in 1819 by Alexander Parris; three years later he had erected a villa in Newport, Rhode Island, designed by George M. Dexter, having rejected one by Isaiah Rogers. This poshest of clients was spreading around the largess, playing the architectural field. The Longwood house is long gone but known in some detail from lists of accounts kept during construction, and by diagrammatic illustrations Shaw published in his *Rural Architecture* of 1843[63] (Fig. 10).

On June 17, 1842, Annie Sears wrote to David that she felt some curiosity "to see the new house, for which 30,000 bricks alone have been expended." At wrote an admiring and admirable analysis of the house as published first in *Rural Architecture*.[64] He wrote, in part, that "the comparison of the [front] elevation with the plan ... shows that the exterior massing was deceptively related to the internal arrangement. The taller, visually dominant section [i.e., shape] ... was quite shallow and housed the service functions. ... The main passage was part of the lower but deeper wing, which houses the formal rooms." The extended external form is a disjointed grouping of smoothly walled blocky shapes beneath gable roofs punctuated by variously sized lancet windows except for the dining-room oriel, and carved bargeboards beneath the eaves. The house, even in perspective projection, is shown in outline with no indication of materials, heft, setting, or shades and shadows.

Shaw published the Sears House as an example of Gothic style in domestic architecture and, perhaps, to crow a little about his distinguished client, whom he names. His perspective of the house falls far short of his own requirement for rendering a design as stated in *Civil Architecture*. And compared to the illustrations of Gothic cottages in contemporary works on domestic architecture, his presentation was behind the times. Set next to the designs published by A. J. Davis in his *Rural Residences* of 1837, by A. J. Downing in his *Cottage Residences* of 1842, or, indeed, in William Bailey Lang's publication on his Downingesque Highland cottages in Roxbury (an area in which Shaw had worked) of 1845,[65] the Sears House was naïve. As we shall see below, Arthur Gilman savaged Shaw's domestic designs in his review of *Rural Architecture*. They were naïve not just in their hesitant use of Gothic stylistic touches, but in the diagrammatic way in which he presented them without the shading in which he drilled his readers in *Civil Architecture*, or ambience, or even an indication of site.

Published House Designs, 1843

The Sears House was one of the series of house designs that first appeared in Shaw's *Rural Architecture* (and were repeated plate for plate in *The Modern Architect*. We will return to these designs in Chapter 3.) He gives a number of domestic projects generated from the orders of classical architecture and details of Gothic. There are eleven houses, including Sears's, one with three variant elevations. Each is shown in plan, main elevation, and unshaded perspective; all appear stuck to the page like pasties. It would seem that only the Sears House was erected from Shaw's designs, but, as we shall see, some of these projects inspired, at least in part, far flung admiration.

The designs, first published in 1843, were intended for upper-middle-class housing to accommodate various-sized American families. His first Grecian Doric design was intended "for a gentleman's residence, in our republican country ... sited atop a gentle eminence." It was to rise from a formal plan to become a three-story rectangular block with two-story colossal porticos. The next is a "very genteel residence," an irregular plan with one-story piazza. Next comes a "cottage, very convenient for a small, genteel family" with "French windows in the piazza." The next repeats the previous description but wraps the French windows in Egyptian frames. This is the single occurrence of an Egyptian motif. The Ionic villa for a village or country town located on the summit of a gentle eminence is intended for comfort and convenience "rarely met in any dwelling." It is a two-story rectangular block with a rear wing, the front elevation centered by a doorway framed by Ionic pilasters "supporting" a low pediment. The Grecian Ionic house of a professional gentleman has a T-shaped plan, an exterior articulated with Doric pilasters, and a one-story, temple-form entrance (see Fig. 24). The next is a slight variation of that. The next provides alternate elevations for one plan, one classical and one which "approaches nearer the ancient English style," that is, Tudor. The Corinthian example is a rectangular, many-roomed mansion with three colossal porticoes, the two on the sides having a column on center. Next comes a cottage made Gothic by lancet windows, over-door labels, and ornamental bargeboards. This is followed by David Sears's Brookline house. Despite his assertion on the title page that his designs were "for the United States of America," some of these plates were copied line for line from an English publication, Samuel H. Brooks's *Designs for Cottage and Villa Architecture* of 1839.

Unidentified Gothic Revival House, 1846

Shaw did a little better, at least with Gothic detailing, in his next known residential commission. Our knowledge of this project comes from a bound set of ten sheets, 10 by 14 inches in ink with a touch of gray wash on Whatman paper, delineating elevations, plans, framing plans, and details signed and dated by Shaw April 21, 1846, on the fourth sheet[66] (Fig. 11). As the elevations are described with compass directions, this must have been prepared for a specific site and hence a specific client. Neither is known. The plan, a variation of some he had published in *Rural Architecture*, is all but symmetrical, with balanced front, or northeast façade, and axial wing extending to the rear. The vocabulary is much as Shaw used for the Sears House, although here the two-story entry block is topped with battlements. Trabeated windows are capped with labels; windows beneath gables are pointed. A detail shows carved bargeboards and the "pinnicle" that slices vertically through the peak of the front gables. Once again Shaw's drawings present the house in elevation without shadows or any indication of ambience.

Houses at Webster Park, West Newton, 1847–48

According to the Massachusetts Historical Commission's National Register Criteria Statement, this residential subdivision was laid out for real estate speculator

Figure 10 Edward Shaw, published perspective of the David Sears II House, Brookline, Massachusetts, 1842–43. Detail of Plate 48 of Shaw's *Rural Architecture* (1843). Author's collection.

that early stage she was somewhat ill informed. There is a long, detailed document containing an estimate for the house dated January 1843, based on the plans as well as another summary list. The exterior was to be of brick and hammered freestone trim. The number of bricks is given as 246,000, whereas 193 perches of cellar stone are itemized. Although stone battlements are mentioned, they do not appear on the house as published in *Rural Architecture* this same year. (The original drawings do not seem to have survived.) Labels above windows are itemized, along with caps and sills, and do appear in Shaw's illustrations. Itemized, too, are slate for the roof and copper for gutters, flashing, and valleys. A fashionable "oriel" or bay window is located in the dining room. The estate came to some $15,000. Shaw's published description of the house gives just $8000, so some reductions in the original plans must have been made, with the published images apparently being the definitive version. In *Rural Architecture* the architect mentions six bedchambers on the upper floor, as well as a "cooking range in the kitchen; bathing-room, water-closet, &c., on the second story; and a Bryant and Herman[n] furnace."

The rooms in the published plans are unlabeled, but on the first floor that to the left front was probably the parlor, that to the left rear the dining room with "oriel," and to the right of the entry the kitchen and its dependencies. Dell Upton

Figure 11 Edward Shaw, *South Easterly Elevation*, unidentified Gothic Revival house, 1846.
Courtesy Historic New England.

William J. Porter by Alexander Wadsworth in 1844. Shaw designed ten nearly
identical neighboring houses with Gothic Revival details for housewright John
Rollins. All have been altered over the years; most now have front piazzas that
may or may not be original. The National Register statement suggests that the
designs might have been taken from Shaw's *Civil Architecture*, but there are no
residential projects in that book, and those in his *Rural Architecture* are not
comparable to these. Rather, Shaw's unidentified Gothic house of the previous
year, with its blocky entrance pavilion and balanced pointed gables (although
in the drawing they are lower than those at Webster Park), seems to have
been the prototype for these houses. Carpenter Gilbert Patter built them. Eight
still stand.

Although as a group the Newton houses represent a rare and significant
collection of Gothic Revival cottages by a known architect, their "gothicness,"
as with the prototype, is mainly confined to details attached to a symmetrical

block, details that have in some cases been removed or altered. The houses all fall far short of being picturesque. Shaw's uncertain handling of Gothic forms led to Arthur Gilman's severe criticism of his *Rural Architecture*, and the intervention of the friends who were responsible for the addition by Thomas W. Silloway and George M. Harding, two much younger architects, of an essay on English Gothic in the sixth edition of *Civil Architecture* (1852). Shaw was a classicist who found it difficult to make the full transition to the picturesque esthetic of midcentury.

ECCLESIASTICAL WORKS

First Unitarian Meeting House, Calais, Maine, 1833–34

The Unitarian Society of Calais originated in 1831. The decision to erect a house of worship came the following year, the cornerstone laid July 12, 1833, and "soon was heard the sound of the carpenter's saw, plane and hammer."[67] According to an article in the *Christian Register* of Boston, a plate in that cornerstone named Edward Shaw of Boston as architect, John Beath as builder, and a building committee of G. I. Galvin, S. S. Shipple, and Isaac Poole. Rev. Win A. Whitewell, a Harvard divinity graduate, led the small congregation at the dedication on May 15, 1834.

The meetinghouse, later the Knight Memorial Methodist Church, is no longer standing, but it is known from a view on a lithographed 1850s wall map of the towns of Calais and St. Stephen, and some vintage photographs (Fig. 12). It appears to have been an earlier, and slightly more imposing, version of the two ecclesiastical designs Shaw was to publish in Plate 51 of his *Rural Architecture* (see Fig. 26). In his discussion of church architecture in that book, he wrote that, in considering the design of a church, one should remember that the "lofty spire, pinnacles, and finals [*sic*], seem as many fingers pointing toward heaven [and] in the massive tower and battlements, the mind perceives an emblem of stability of truth, and of the gracious promises of God." For the prototype in Calais of those published designs, he used a four-bay gabled hall lighted by triple-lancet windows and fronted by a tower that rose into a belfry topped by a spire accompanied by corner pinnacles. An axial Tudor archway, triple-lancet window, and quatrefoil opening in the belfry were stacked beneath the crenellations crowning both stages of the tower. The result here was somewhat more imposing than those of his published designs, where he added a clock above the main lancet.

The church at Calais spawned variations of itself, including, in neighboring East Machais, Maine, the First Congregational Church of 1836 by "designer" and builder John Ellis Seavey (1810–87), (Fig. 13) and in Machias in the Centre

Figure 12   Edward Shaw, First Unitarian Meeting House, Calais, Maine, 1833–34. From Calais and St. Stephen map, Philadelphia: E. M. Woodford, 1856. Courtesy of Old Sturbridge Village Research Library.

Street Congregational Church of 1837. Perhaps an even closer spawn was the Congregational Church in Orford, New Hampshire, completed in 1854. Drawings for the building by Moses Gerrish Wood are dated 1851. Moved to Norwich, Vermont, in 1863, it was destroyed by fire in 1917. A replica now stands in its place.[68] The same published images may lie loosely behind the design for the Episcopal Church that once stood on State Street in Springfield, Massachusetts.[69] What Shaw and his followers did not carry over to later ecclesiastical designs were the half-octagonal piers and buttresses he used in Calais, but he would

41

Figure 13 John Ellis Seavey, First Congregational Church, East Machias, Maine, 1836. Photograph 1975. Courtesy Historic New England.

return to those piers at his Town Hall for Manchester, New Hampshire, and a third church design he first published in the 1850 edition of *Rural Architecture,* and elsewhere (see Fig. 27).

Malden Centre Methodist Church, Massachusetts, 1842

The "Second Church" of the Malden Methodists rose on the corner of Pleasant and Waverly streets on land purchased from Samuel Cox. Commenced in July

1842, during the pastorate of George Landon, it was dedicated on October 20th. Joseph Lewis and Oakman Joyce of Medford erected it from Edward Shaw's design.[70] Its original dimensions were $63^1/2$ by 46 feet, but it was enlarged in 1855 and enriched with a 137-foot steeple from the design of Harvey Graves of Boston in 1873. The building was superseded by another built on a different site designed by George A. Clough that was destroyed by fire three years later.[71] Judging by available visual documentation, Shaw's church was a simple rectangular box with gable roof articulated by pilasters separating large trabeated windows. The National Register application calls it Greek Revival but that is a generous designation. This church was apparently nothing like the ecclesiastical designs Shaw would publish the next year in *Rural Architecture*.

Published Church Designs, 1843

In *Rural Architecture*, 1843, Shaw published designs (Plates 51–52), presumably his own, for two Gothic churches. He added a third for the 1850 edition; they all reappeared in *The Modern Architect*. (The Italianate design in the sixth edition of *Civil Architecture* [1852] was presumably the work of Silloway and Harding.) The first two were intended for a village or country town. Shaw's description in the text particularly points out the "Tudor flowers" at the eaves and the trefoils and quatrefoils on the tower, as well as the provision for a school room in the basement of the larger church. His third design is a more elaborate version more extensively detailed of the same parti, with half-octagon piers and busier spire. As noted above, the first two reverberated through Shaw's later projects and were echoed in small country churches throughout New England.[72]

PENAL DESIGN

House of Correction, Middlesex County, Massachusetts, 1837, 1839

In early 1837, the Middlesex County Commissioners asked Shaw to draw up a house of correction for the site of the overcrowded prison designed by Charles Bulfinch in 1813 and erected 1814–16. That was a three-story, hipped-roof, granite building 95 by 45 feet at Third and Spring streets in East Cambridge. The Commissioners debated whether to build an addition to the existing structure or replace it.[73] By April, Shaw had completed a portfolio of twelve drawings—plans, elevations, sections, and details now at Historic New England—for a prison to replace completely the old one. The proposed outer shell was an austere four-story granite block fitting the footprint of Bulfinch's building, with a monitor silhouette. Within were four floors of stone cell blocks, each containing twenty-four narrow cells, the whole kept well back from the outer walls as was the standard of security practice in prison design of the era. The block included a kitchen, bathing room, chapel, keeper's room, and storeroom.

The portfolio also contains several sheets of detailed specifications, among them, outer walls were to be of single stones one-and-a-half-foot thick, each pinned to its neighbors above, below, and to the sides with six dowels; floors and ceilings of four-inch mica slate with edges laid into the walls; cast-iron bars on the windows let into holes drilled into the stone; cast-iron cell and other doors, and so on. There is a final N.B.: Although Shaw thought the dowels in the walls were "indispensable" for security, he mentions that Rev. Louis Dwight, the prison reformer with whom he had just collaborated on a competition entry for the New York Halls of Justice, "thinks them entirely useless" given the "present mode of supervision," and eliminating them would save much on expenses. Shaw left the decision up to the commissioner's "opinion."

The proposal to replace completely the old jail seemed too costly to the Commissioners, so in June 1839 Shaw produced another portfolio of nine drawings, these too in the collection at Historic New England, in which he connected a slightly smaller but equally ominous version of his previous design with monitor by means of a one-story wing to the existing hipped-roof prison. His "Description" focuses closely on the construction of the cells for which he prescribes walls of "good hard" brick. He envisions them "in the clear 7 feet deep [that is, long] 7 feet high, 3 f 6 in. wide," with walls from sixteen- to twenty-inches thick. (Presently incarcerated offenders might contemplate those coffin-like spaces in which prisoners remained alone for most of the time.) "The opening through the doors for light and air are valuable considerations," Shaw wrote, "and should be as large as the security of the cells would admit of." The commissioners accepted this second proposal and paid Shaw $190 for both sets plus $12 for laying out the foundation lines at the site. The *Salem Gazette* noted in July of the next year that $30,000 had been budgeted for the building, which opened in 1839. Shaw's wing survived the demolition of Bulfinch's jailhouse in 1872, but vanished in 1965.

COMPETITION LOSSES

City Hall, Albany, New York, 1829

Announced through the press in June 1829, the competition was meant to find the best design for the new civic building "to consist of a high basement and two stories of appropriate height." Floor plans, elevations, and at least one section were required. By the end of July the committee had in hand twenty-four sets of drawings. The premium was split between local architect, Philip Hooker, and John Kutts of Boston. Shaw's design, certainly one of his earliest, failed to make the final group; his drawings have never come to light.[74]

Masonic Temple, Boston, 1830

In June 1830, the Boston Masons appointed among their members a building committee for their new temple, one that included the architect Joseph Jenkins, who was to endorse Shaw's *Civil Architecture* in this period. They acquired a lot on Tremont Street opposite the Common, and "then employed architects to draw plans of the proposed Temple, and procured several models from which they selected and adopted that according to which the Temple has been built."[75] The design chosen was the work of Isaiah Rogers, himself a Mason. Shaw, apparently not a brother, numbered among the other unknown competitors. An unsigned article about his design in the *Boston Traveler* in 1832 reports that author's reaction to Rogers's building.[76] He found it as a whole "a very elegant structure . . . but there is something about it which does not suffer it to repose upon the eye as a work of perfect harmony . . . for which we could only . . . account, by supposing that there had been a deviation from the original design, to accommodate expense or convenience." (The writer was not alone in his criticism of the realized building.[77]) He goes on to say that he has seen "the first plan, drawn by Mr. Shaw," which he did not hesitate to say "is one of the best designs we have ever seen in the course of our acquaintance with architectural elegance." Although he understood that the Masons were "highly pleased with the plan" (Shaw's planning was invariably praised in the local press), they laid it aside for reasons of which he is ignorant. "Had it been erected, it would have been the finest pile of architecture in America [!]." He added: "To those whose future convenience may require a plan for a gothic structure, combining harmony, sober dignity, and classic elegance, we recommend . . . Mr. Edward Shaw, Architect, No. 4 North Russell street, Boston." (In that description our anonymous critic seems to have unknowingly prescribed Shaw's design for the Town House in Manchester, New Hampshire, as we shall see, of more than a decade later.)

Girard College, Philadelphia, 1832

When the banker and philanthropist Stephen Girard died at the end of 1831 he left a will in which he provided up to two million dollars to be used to erect "a permanent College, with suitable out-buildings, sufficiently spacious for the residence and accommodation of at least three hundred scholars. . . . The said College shall be constructed with the most durable materials . . . [and] avoid needless ornament, [with attention given] chiefly to the strength, convenience, and neatness of the whole [Girard obviously knew his Vitruvius]. . . . It shall be three stories in height, each story at least fifteen feet high. . . . It shall be fireproof inside and outside." And so on for page after page of minute specifications covering nearly every inch of the intended school. In June 1832, the building committee announced a competition for the design to conform to Girard's will, and by the end of the year seventeen projects of varied stature had arrived.[78] In early February of 1833 Thomas U. Walter's design was awarded first prize, followed by entries from William Strickland and Isaiah Rogers.

Edward Shaw was among the also-ran competitors. Given the above timeline he must have drawn his entry between the announcement in June and the due date in December. We know it from the set of seven sheets of drawings preserved in the Girard College History Collections. All are ink and wash on Whatman paper and larger than the sheets he used for domestic designs at 19 by 24 inches. They include

1. Front and side elevations of the main and out buildings.
2. Elevation of the College furnished with marble pilasters and plan of wall and portico.
3. Side elevation of College with pilasters, plan of wall with pilasters.
4. Ground-floor plan of main and outbuildings.
5. Plan of second floor of main and outbuildings.
6. Third and fourth floors of the four corner buildings and the third of the center [main] one.
7. Longitudinal and transverse cross-sections of main and outbuildings.

The overall layout was a five-spot arrangement of four smaller rectangular dormitories in the corners and the larger school building in the center (Fig. 14). They were to be of brick with marble embellishments.

In the definitive study of the competition, Michael J. Lewis remarks that Shaw was more at home in wood and proved himself timid in handling monumental masonry forms. The architect's *Operative Masonry*, published the year of the competition, demonstrated his vast knowledge of brick and stone construction if not monumental proportions. His drawings suggest that he produced them in a hurry.[79] "He was," wrote Lewis, "the only first-rate architect in the competition who turned in a second-rate performance." It may be that the stiffness of his drawings, compared to the renderings of Walter and Strickland, who were indeed better artists than Shaw, derived in part from what he wrote on his cover sheet for his entry: "In preparing the following Plan," he stated, "the strictest attention has been given to the letter of the Will." Winners are not always those who follow the rules. Because, as Lewis also points out, Shaw's layout of the ancillary buildings suggests that he forgot he was planning for eight-years-olds, it is fair to recognize that, although he was the oldest entrant, so far as we know Shaw

Figure 14 Edward Shaw, Elevation of Girard College Main Building (competition entry), Philadelphia, Pennsylvania, 1832. Courtesy of Girard College History Collections, Philadelphia PA.

had not previously attempted a design for such a large and complicated program as that for the College. But it must also be said that his project for the Custom House in Boston of some five years later, though better drawn, hardly yet demonstrated complete ease with the details of monumental design in the era of granite Grecian popularity.

New York Halls of Justice (The Tombs), 1835

After months of discussion about erecting a prison in New York City, a competition was announced in late January 1835. The building was to "comprise a Prison for two hundred offenders committed to trial—a Prison for fifty debtors—a Common Court Room, Grand and Petit Jury Rooms—etc., etc.; a Police Office and Watch House."[80] An elaborate list of "Instructions to Architects" followed. Drawings were to be in the hands of the committee in three weeks! Some sixty hopefuls answered the call; twenty-five submitted proposals. On March 7 the committee picked John Haviland's Egyptian Revival design. In third place was an entry by Dwight and Shaw, so far as is known the only time the architect placed in a major competition, which was praised for its "Kitchen, Chappel [sic], [and] Supervision," the latter presumably referring to an arrangement for guarding the

47

inmates. As we noted earlier, Rev. Louis Dwight of Boston, was, among other things, a well-known prison reformer. He served for many years as secretary of the Massachusetts Society for Prison Discipline, whose object was "to promote the improvement of public Prisons." When it was formed there was "hardly a prison which was not a disgrace to any civilized land; now there are several which might serve ... as models to the world."[81] He was, we know, a consultant for Shaw's design of the Middlesex County House of Correction, and is known to have worked with other architects, among them Gridley J. F. Bryant, in proposing his ideas for buildings such as prisons and almshouses.[82] The Dwight–Shaw entry has not come to light, nor has a description beyond that given by the judges of the competition.

U. S. Custom House, Boston, 1837

Once the site for the Custom House had been established and paid for by August 1837, and an earlier design for a different site by an unknown architect declared unsuitable in October, the call went out in the newspapers for drawings. The only competitors known by name, other than Shaw, were Thomas Cully of Philadelphia, Frederick Catherwood, Richard Upjohn (perhaps), and the winner, Ammi B. Young. It would seem that federal government competitions were then often badly managed, with competitors in the dark about procedures.[83] On February 6, 1838, Shaw "wrote an exasperated letter to Levi Woodbury, Secretary of the Treasury, wanting to know just who was to cast the deciding vote regarding selection of the best design."[84] Would it be someone in Boston or Washington? Having heard of "one of the Architects of Boston who had submitted a plan to the Commissioners of the new Custom House, [he] is thinking about taking a copy of the same to Washington." Shaw asked where he should send his plans to receive "an equally fair hearing," but he is certain justice would be done. The Commissioners chose A. B. Young's design, which included models, on February 21. Little known Thomas Cully was the runner-up.

Shaw's project is preserved at the Boston Public Library in a bound portfolio of eight drawings on 16½-by-22-inch wove paper plus a written "Description" dated December 30, 1837[85] (Fig. 15). He called for fireproofing by brick arched ceilings and brick floors, with cast-iron doors and shutters in the interior side of the walls. His overall design was similar in concept to Young's, a cruciform plan topped by a dome, but much less impressive. Instead of the winner's sweeping staircases leading to the main entrances on the second level, Shaw drew unaccentuated doors and windows at ground level. The rather attenuated proportions of the twenty-eight colossal Corinthian columns of Shaw's four porticos are reminiscent of Bulfinch's Federal State House, and lack the boldness of Young's Grecian Doric order. The half-generation between their ages may be

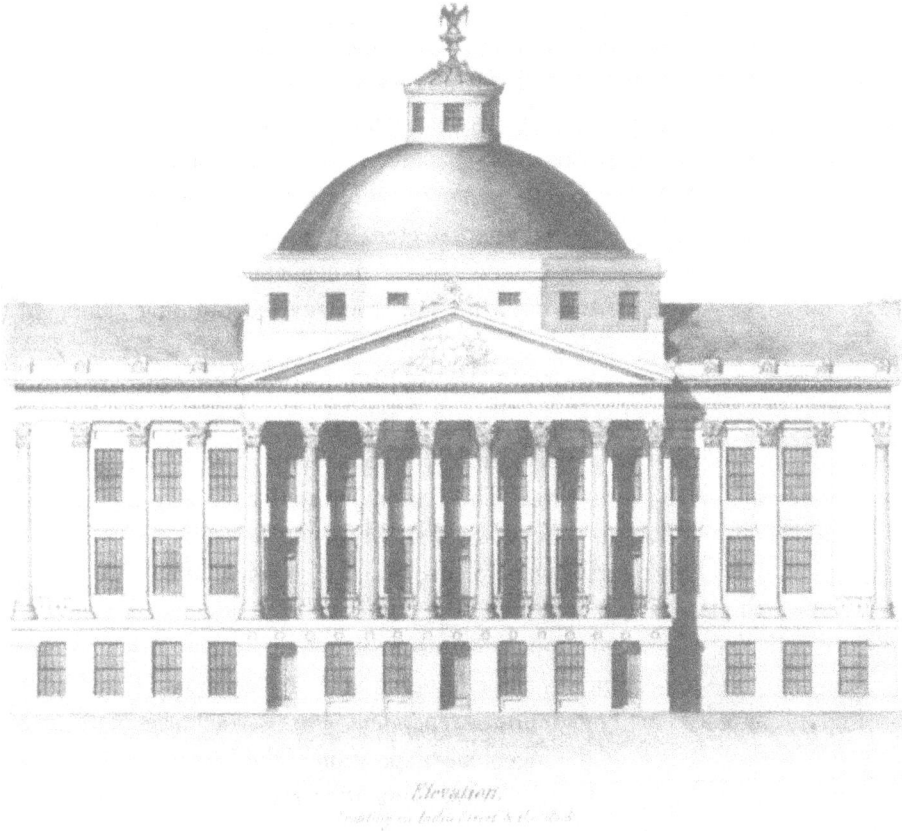

Figure 15 Edward Shaw, *Elevation Fronting on India Street & the Dock*, U. S. Custom House (competition entry), Boston, Massachusetts, 1837. Courtesy of the Trustees of the Boston Public Library, Rare Books Department.

seen here. Young's large geometrical shapes are allowed to speak for themselves, whereas Shaw embellished his pediments and lunettes with classical and figurative carvings. The oculus of Young's dome forms a compact low profile at the crown of the vault, whereas Shaw proposed a two-shelled dome topped with an eight-windowed observatory poking up from the outer crest. It is reminiscent of what he placed on his contemporary Thaxter House. He perched an eagle atop that. While Young created one of the canonical images of the Grecian Revival era, Shaw's concept was rooted in the passé, Federal Style, Roman-based classicism of the turn of the century. This was not because he did not know how to detail the Grecian style. He had been publishing Grecian elements in *Civil Architecture* for a number of years, and his contemporary frontispiece for the same Beacon Hill house demonstrated that he could engage in the present on a smaller scale with fine results. Larger concepts eluded him.

State Capitol, Columbus, Ohio, 1838

A new capitol for Ohio was authorized by the legislature in late January 1838, and notice of the fact went out to the newspapers.[86] A letter in April gave detailed specifications, including square footage, materials, and site. The Grecian Doric order was recommended but not demanded. Some fifty or sixty designs were submitted, although the exact number is unknown and the architects' names are mostly lost. The prizewinner was selected in October. In 1839, A. J. Davis combined elements of the placed entries into a composite, which was itself modified, that became the basis for the often revised building campaign that lasted into the early 1860s.

Shaw's design has never surfaced, and the fact that he drew one has never been recognized until now. We know he did submit a proposal, as well as learn about other of his lost projects, from the newspapers. Shaw seems to have had the attention of the local press. The *Boston Transcript* for May 15, 1839, ran a notice about the premium recently rewarded for the best plan of the Ohio State Capitol. "We have seen several plans, sent from this quarter," we read, "but none which pleases us more than one by Mr. Shaw. The style is Grecian [perhaps in reaction to his failed project for the Boston Custom House of the previous year], and the appearance of the edifice on such a plan must be highly impos-ing. . . . We could not but admire, independent of the correct taste of the architect in the general structure, the ingenious disposition of the Legislative Halls, Secretary, Treasurer's, and Clerks' offices, Committee rooms, &c, &c, which are all sufficiently numerous, large, commodious, and well lighted, leaving large space for areas, corridors, and free ventilation. The plan is worth examining." This was not the only time that the press praised Shaw's skill in planning. The whereabouts of the drawings thus described are unknown.

Boston Athenaeum, 1845

In 1845 a committee of the Trustees of the Boston Athenaeum, a Brahmin proprietary library and art gallery, offered an astonishing $1,000 premium for the best plan of a building to be erected on Tremont Street. The circular, dated January 25th, contains a detailed description of the site and the program, which included income-producing shops on Tremont (although that proposed invasion of commerce into culture did not sit well with some members). It did not recommend a style. A number of architects entered the anonymous competition; George M. Dexter won the prize with an Italianate design. When his project proved too expensive the next year the Trustees called for a new competition for a building on Beacon Street. Edward Clarke Cabot won that second competition with a building whose Palladian façade still stands.[87] The Athenaeum retains many of the competitive designs, including that for the first site attributed to Edward

Figure 16   Attributed to Edward Shaw, Boston Athenaeum, Tremont Street and Court Square elevations (competition entry for first site), 1845. Courtesy of the Boston Athenaeum.

Shaw (he apparently did not try again) on the basis of its similarity to his design for the Town Hall, Manchester, New Hampshire, of the roughly same date.[88] There are six plans on three sheets and two elevations on a single sheet (Fig. 16).

The originally intended site sloped a full story from Tremont Street to Court Square. In what looks like Shaw's preliminary layout, the ground floor of the Tremont section seems given over to shops with a central entrance providing access to a straight corridor leading to the stairway and then, at the same level, to the second floor of the Court Square block and a statuary loft. (The circular had suggested as much.) The first floor on the lower Court Square also was to have a corridor leading straight from the entrance, between statuary displays to the central stair. So there were to be entries opposite one another, one in each principal façade, but a different levels. The second floor on Tremont is labeled "reading room" and the third floor rear was to contain the library. The third floor on Tremont was intended for library or hall with galleries, whereas the fourth level on Court would hold the picture gallery. These two sheets, one in pencil, both with lettering in script, seem more like preliminary sketches than serious entries in a $1,000-prize contest. (Catherina Slautterback points to another drawing preserved at the Athenaeum that was "obviously not intended for presentation.")

Shaw, as did other competitors, broke his definitive plan into two parts joined by a central stairway. On the third sheet of plans, containing his developed proposal, Shaw used all of the given lot, as the circular demanded, by splaying the sides of his building to conform to the irregular property lines, something

51

the plans of other entrants also followed. The diagrams on this sheet are better presented in ink but lack room designations. The shops would seem to have vanished, although the corridor off Tremont straight to the main stair remains, avoiding the areas of plan left and right, the use of which is not at all clear. Of what is preserved of Shaw's project only this plan and the elevations reach the level of presentation of which Shaw was capable.

His elevations far outshine his plans; they appear in delicate, accomplished drawings and they stand out stylistically from those of other known competitors. Following the trend of the time, theirs were generally Italianate. Shaw's presumptive entry, on the other hand, exhibits his personal rendering of Gothic detail on a basically classical framework. There are two five-bay elevations: one with an attic story between lancets and crenellations and one without. They are otherwise identical. One assumes (they have no titles) that these are the façades on Court Square and Tremont Street, respectively, and that the larger drawing depicts the taller Court Square face, which Shaw seems to have thought of as the main front. In each of these elevations there is only a central entrance leading into the buildings. Tall half-octagon pilasters set upon elongated pedestals and topped by pinnacles divided the wall into bays. These are opened by square windows at the ground level. Above each bay are three narrow, two-story lancets set into trabeated frames surmounted by labels. The Court Square face has a frieze of quatrefoils inserted above the main fenestration. Both walls are crested with another ornamental frieze and decorative crenellations. Two boxy skylights, echoing the treatment below, their corners edged by spiky pinnacles, ride the hip roof; they were intended to provide light to the circular stairs below.

These elevations derive from Shaw's design for the slightly earlier Town Hall in Manchester, New Hampshire (see Fig. 19). Similar too are the sides of the most ornamental of the three churches he published in *Rural Architecture* (see Fig. 26). The façade of the Hatch Hotel on Main Street in Bangor, Maine, of the 1850s is so similar that it should also be attributed to him (Fig. 17), as should the contemporary front of the store housing Freeman Orne, Dealer in Gutta Percha, at 125-27 Hanover Street in Boston.

Deer Island Almshouse Hospital, 1849

The 1847 outbreak of cholera in Boston instituted a long campaign to build a free city hospital, at first in a temporary building on Deer Island in the harbor. In 1849 the city promised a prize for the best design for an "almshouse," which was to be in fact a quarantine station and hospital for (mostly Irish) newcomers. That was eventually erected from the design of Gridley J. F. Bryant in collaboration with the Rev. Louis Dwight.[89] Although the names of other aspirants are not known, it is now certain that Edward Shaw submitted a design, one that was

Figure 17 Attributed to Edward Shaw, Hatch Hotel, Bangor, Maine, ca. 1850. Courtesy of Earle G. Shettleworth, Jr.

praised by the medical profession. *The Boston Medical and Surgical Journal* for July 4, 1849, announced the beginning of the competition, for which there will "be no lack of competitors." It had already studied "with peculiar satisfaction" Shaw's proposal, but held no hope for its acceptance. "As he always has met with a rebuff in all attempts for the patronage of the city government, the same course of neglect may be expected on this occasion; but the merit of having devised a plan of a beautiful and excellent arrangement of apartments, appropriate in every respect for the purposes specified, will belong to him, and it will be unfortunate for the city if his economical scheme is not adopted. Some clumsy affair, the offspring of a cousin's cousin, it is presumed, will receive the smile of fortune, or, what is the same thing, the approval of a majority of the building committee." Seven days later the *Transcript* noted the medical journal's endorsement of Shaw's design, and, although it could not address its comparative merits, judged "the commendation to be very just . . . [for] this plan is certainly a very fine one; combining elegance and convenience, with provision for the ample accommodation of 2000 persons." As with Shaw's project for the Connecticut

State Capitol, this scheme was praised for its adroit layout. The drawings these writers described have not been located.

A COMPETITION WON

Town House (Later City Hall), Manchester, New Hampshire, 1844–45

When in August of 1844 the three-year-old Town House at Manchester burned, Town Meeting voted to replace it as soon as possible, "as good, or better, . . . and put a clock and bell, on the same."[90] A building committee was appointed to furnish a plan, and, in conjunction with the Selectmen, named Elijah Hanson as agent to oversee the project. "They have authority to receive proposals, and to let it to the one proposing to build it on the most advantageous terms," according to the *Manchester American* for September 6, 1844. A week later the same paper reported the result of what was probably a kind of quick, informal competition. It said, "Several plans for the new Town House have been obtained by the committee. The plan of Mr. Shaw has been adopted. It is beautiful beyond measure." No other competitor is named. Two weeks later the paper announced that sealed proposals for rebuilding the Town House according to the winning plan and specifications would be accepted until October 6. It should be noted that the same day the paper carried an ad for Shaw's latest publication, his *Rural Architecture* of 1843, for sale by a local book dealer.

Although Shaw's New Hampshire birth might have boosted his chances of winning, according to S. D. Bell's *A History of Manchester* (1845), his design was chosen for "the beauty of its architecture, convenience of its plan, and durability of the structure." (He, like other writers we have quoted, must have had access to a copy of Vitruvius.) He goes on to say that "the architecture is unique, being similar to the Gothic, but not exactly of that order." He was not the only onlooker perplexed by Shaw's creation. The building was far different from what the town might have expected, something more Grecian, perhaps, like Isaiah Rogers's contemporary building for Quincy, Massachusetts, but to its credit, if it could not put a name to the style, it could recognize the merit of a fresh amalgamation of classical form and Gothic detail. The building was finished by late 1845 or early 1846 at the cost of $35,000 (Fig. 18). It may have been the public building Shaw referred to as costing $40,000 in his comment about his career published in *The Modern Architect.*

The construction, at Elm and Market streets, which quickly became a City Hall, included a basement post office. The city clerk, mayor, assessors, and other offices occupied the second floor. The third accommodated a council chamber. Originally, and as recently rehabilitated, the main entrance gives access to the

Figure 18 Edward Shaw, Town (now part of City) Hall, Manchester, New Hampshire, 1844–45. Vintage photo ca. 1870 courtesy of Earle G. Shettleworth, Jr.

stair in the tower. The most noteworthy feature of the original plan was the accommodation for five shops on the ground floor leased to a drug store, insurance agency, bank, and other enterprises. The combination of commercial and governmental usage in one building was at least as old in New England as Faneuil Hall in Boston. The appearance of Shaw's *Rural Architecture* in Manchester at the time of the selection of Shaw's design for the Town House is one of those fortuitous coincidences of history. Plate 51 of that book depicts the front elevations of two Gothic churches "for a village or country town" (see Fig. 26). As Richard Candee pointed out long ago, not only government buildings but churches might also contain ground-floor shops (despite Christ's driving of the money changers from the temple).[91] Combining features of his two freshly published church designs and adding a few flourishes, Shaw arrived at the overall form of his Manchester Town Hall.

Original plans and specifications do not seem to have survived, but C. E. Potter, who in his slightly later history of the town calls the building "of a very

Figure 19   Edward Shaw, Town (now part of City) Hall, Manchester. Side elevation. Photo: author, 2015.

peculiar style of architecture, nothing of the classical or pure about it, but still a fine looking structure," goes on to say that Shaw proposed a building "entirely of stone, the columns hammered and the wall of ashlar work; but the committee deviated from his plan, and the building is of stone and brick, the columns and caps being of hammered stone, while the walls are of brick, painted and sanded to imitate stone" (Fig. 19). The report of the selectmen for 1844–45 lists $75 paid to Shaw for his plan, $227 for "first floor," $700 for "advancement," $500 for "advancement," and another $700 for "advancement." Clearly, he closely supervised construction.

The exterior of the Town Hall recalls other contemporary projects by Shaw, including the flanking elevations for the Boston Athenaeum of the following year. In addition, a hotel in Bangor, Maine, and a shop in Boston also reflected Shaw's design.

The building has captured the admiring attention of later commentators. Among the most enthusiastic was John Coolidge, who wrote, "the whole is spiced with delightful Gothic detail, octagonal buttresses, bands of quatrefoils, battlements, tracery, all those favorite forms culled from [Augustus] Pugin's *Specimens* [*of Gothic Architecture*, 1821–23]. But while the application is anything but Gothic, it is nowise haphazard. . . . Here, as in the best early romantic buildings, the new discovery does not run away with the designer. At bottom there remains a splendid sense of proportions and of the relationship of masses, while the detail merely gives a needed touch of fantasy to the severe regularity of the scheme." In a note, Coolidge credits Lewis Mumford with observing that the windows here are large, whereas "most Gothic Revival buildings tended to reduce the window area."[92] By the time of his last known building Shaw had found an original way to merge his earlier classicism with the seemingly opposite newcomer.[93]

3

BOOKS

Of more lasting value than his drawings or buildings in the study of the history of nineteenth-century American architecture are Shaw's books. They also have their place in the history of American book publishing. He issued five separate titles. It is best to say *titles* rather than *books*, for his three works devoted mainly to architecture are largely variants of the same book (although *Rural Architecture* and *The Modern Architect* are much closer to each other than any edition of *Civil Architecture* is to them), as are his two works on masonry materials and methods (Hitchcock gives the two only one complete entry[94]). Shaw or his publishers tinkered somewhat with content and illustrations, revising or extending text or replacing some plates and changing format, especially in the several versions of *Civil Architecture*, the sixth edition of which was largely reworked by two younger architects (see #11, below), but similarities persist through them all. The same could be said of multiple works published by Shaw's American competitors.

There was then no publisher who specialized in architectural books. Shaw's titles, like those of his slightly older contemporary, Asher Benjamin, were often issued by booksellers who were also publishers of popular works such as religious biography, tracts, and sermons. The physical appearance of his books reflects the changes in bookmaking in the United States from the 1830s into the 1850s.[95] Like other publications of the era, Shaw's texts were letterpress set by hand on wove paper. The full-page intaglio illustrations on plate paper were invariably said to be engravings on copper. Most copies examined for this study proved to be from mildly to heavily foxed, including later editions in which tissue was laid over engravings. Grained English cloth binding began to replace leather (or "calf") in this country in the 1820s, although half, full, or quarter leather with or without leather corners can be found on some copies of Shaw's books into the 1840s. Spines of later copies bear gold-stamped labels; some editions of *Civil Architecture* read SHAW'S / ARCHITECT [*sic*] on the spine and *Shaw's Civil Architecture* on the title page (Fig. 20). Such a combination of the possessive of an author's last name and one or two words of the title was commonly used on books of this period.

By the 1830s, at the beginning of Shaw's publishing career, binderies were producing cased books in cloth covers with labels of printed paper or stamped leather on front covers or spines. By the 1840s, embossed decorative patterns appeared, as did machine-stamped gilt or blind-stamped central cover vignettes and embossed borders. Ornamental dies cut by engravers proliferated, some title specific, some cut for general use. Marbled end papers and fore edges appeared on many works. Shaw's later editions show all these characteristics. Some binders and engravers signed their work, although no such identification appears on books examined for this study. Unfortunately, no information about the sizes of Shaw's editions has come to light.

No. 14

$72

CIVIL ARCHITECTURE:

OR

A COMPLETE THEORETICAL AND PRACTICAL

SYSTEM OF BUILDING,

CONTAINING

THE FUNDAMENTAL PRINCIPLES OF THE ART,

WITH

THE FIVE ORDERS OF ARCHITECTURE.

ALSO A GREAT VARIETY OF EXAMPLES

SELECTED FROM

VITRUVIUS, STUART, CHAMBERS, AND NICHOLSON;

WITH

MANY USEFUL AND ELEGANT ORNAMENTS,

AND RULES FOR PROJECTING THEM

ILLUSTRATED WITH NINETY-SEVEN COPPERPLATE ENGRAVINGS.

BY EDWARD SHAW, ARCHITECT.

SECOND EDITION,

REVISED AND ENLARGED.

BOSTON:
PUBLISHED BY MARSH, CAPEN & LYON.

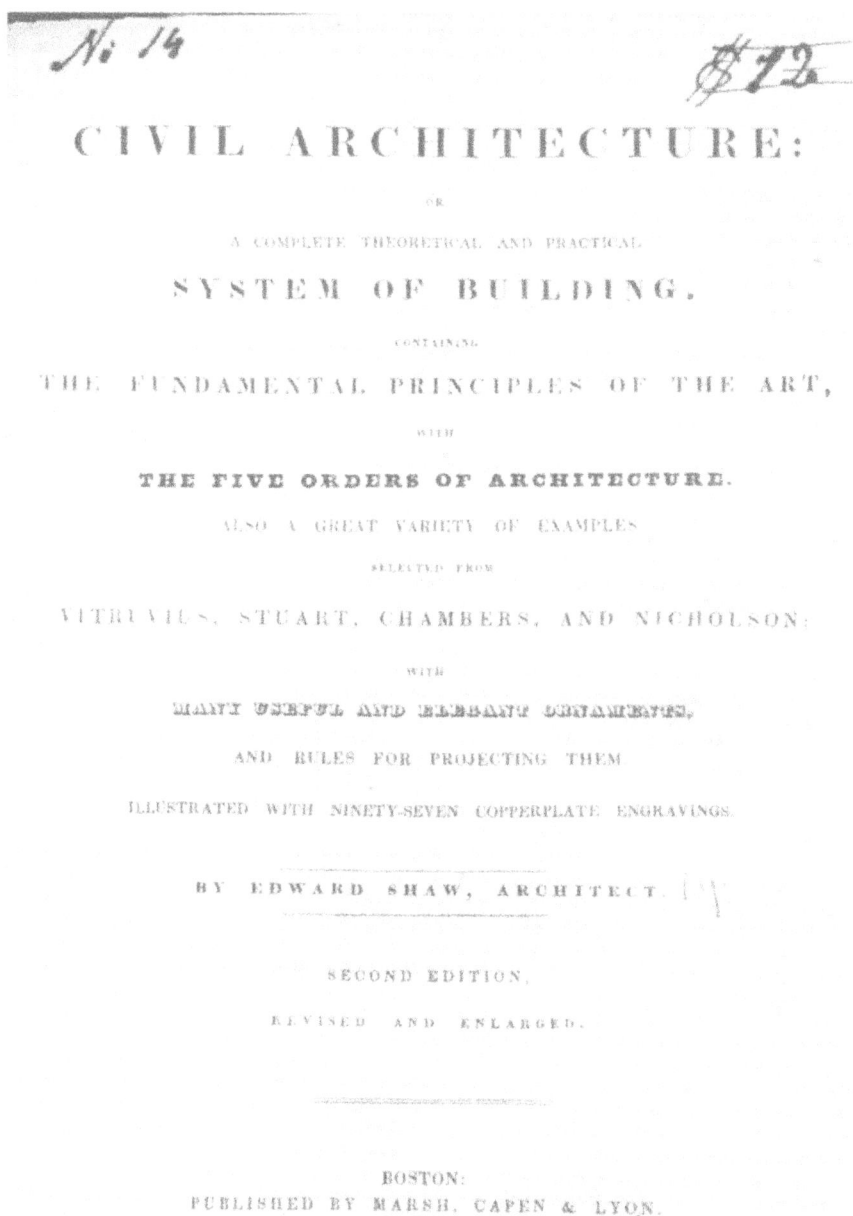

Figure 20   Edward Shaw, title page to *Civil Architecture*, second edition, Boston: Marsh, Capen & Lyon, 1832. Author's collection.

Shaw's books came in a variety of bindings, ranging from simple to decorative. Few contemporary observations about this come down to us, but there was obviously a range of designs to appeal to a range of buyers or users (they were not, apparently, always the same). Where original bindings survive, some of the earlier ones are full or quarter leather with stamped titles on the front cover or labels on the squared-off spine; some are plain cloth with no exterior identification or with paper or leather printed labels on the spine. Eventually, some appeared embossed with an overall filigree and a gold-stamped scene on the front cover, perhaps a blind stamp on the back, and ornamental decorations on the cased spine. Because Boston was one of the three leading publishing centers in the country (the others were New York and Philadelphia), local printers, engravers, and binders were plentiful. Benjamin Bradley, the Bostonian who founded one of the first cloth binderies in the country, worked for many of the local publishers between the 1830s and the 1850s, although the appearance of none of Shaw's works is now attributed to him.

It seems that not all versions of Shaw's publications were intended to go to work in the hands of on-site mechanics. At first, *Civil Architecture* was primarily a builder's guide aimed at the fledgling operative. Its early presentation in simple calf bindings said as much, but copies of the "revised and improved" sixth edition (1852) were bound in ornamental covers. This appeared as a two-inch thick, four-pound quarto with marbled end papers and fore edges; that is, hardly primarily intended to be used at or easily portable to the work site. Without forgetting the mechanic, Shaw produced in his later titles a series of house and church designs primarily aimed at the consuming public. Those volumes—*Rural Architecture* and *The Modern Architect*—are style books usually dressed up in ornamental bindings. When *Rural Architecture* appeared with a gold-stamped Nativity scene on the front cover (an example of the use of a stock die unrelated to the subject of the book) and a pictorial spine with a composition of builders' tools and a slender church spire, it was said by one reviewer to be "as ornamental as useful." The handsomely decorated spines of some copies of Shaw's works on architecture suggest that they were in fact intended for home study by aspiring architects and builders as well as to stand impressively on a bibliophile's book shelf, or, as was urged by a reviewer, that "of every liberal gentleman and scholar."[96]

In contrast, in the same year Shaw's *Rural Architecture* first appeared (1843), Benjamin B. Mussey put out Asher Benjamin's *The Architect, or Practical House Carpenter* in a plain calf binding. This seems to have been generally characteristic of Benjamin's books. Copies of the books examined for this study were mostly calf, quarter calf, or plain cloth. Some had simple gold-stamped titles. Obviously, Benjamin and his publishers did not assume as broad a range of buyers as did Shaw and his. The one exception to this generalization noted during this study is Benjamin's octavo *Elements of Architecture* (1843) published by Benjamin B. Mussey, who issued Shaw's *Rural Architecture* in the same year (see #8, below). The 1849 edition of the *Elements* appeared in embossed cloth with a gold-stamped spine ornamented with a drawing of an oriel window. It is a work different in size and content from Benjamin's other books. Hitchcock notes that it was the last of his seven titles, and the least popular.

Although there was little critical notice in the press given to Shaw's publications during his lifetime (except, as we shall see, for Arthur Gilman's nefarious, ad hominem blasting of *Rural Architecture*), there were a series of solicited positive endorsements from his peers on the arrival of *Civil Architecture*. And there are other ways of measuring Shaw's place on architects', builders', and others' library shelves. As seen below, copies signed by owners were broadly distributed across the country late into the century. These signatures substantiate Talbot Hamlin's statement that "it was in the East that the important architectural books by Asher Benjamin, Edward Shaw, and Minard LaFever originated. Yet with what enthusiasm the builders and designers of the Northwest Territories played with these influences."[97] Such marginalia is of course hit or miss information based on accessible copies of his work examined during a limited period of time.[98] One could never find every inscribed copy of his books, but the physical examination for this study of many examples in public and private collections found a spread from Maine, New Hampshire, Massachusetts, Rhode Island, and Connecticut, to New York, New Jersey, and South Carolina, then to Ohio, Indiana, Illinois, and Michigan as well as Arkansas and Texas. One bookplate gives us Kentucky, whereas the distribution suggested by newspaper notices adds Tennessee and Missouri. And finally there is the evidence of architectural details copied from his plates, which can be found in buildings as far away as the West Coast. Marginalia, handwritten critical comments on the text, or other marks of ownership such as sketches, have proven to be somewhat scarce. No author presentation copies have yet surfaced.

Men of the past who signed their copies of Shaw's books—as expected most are men, although a few women's names do appear—become real to us through their handwritten or stamped claims of ownership. (Although ownership does not guarantee readership, it does track distribution.) The signers uncovered in this study include architects, builders, joiners, carpenters, masons, housewrights, surveyors, businessmen, real estate brokers, manufacturers, lawyers, ministers, university libraries, mechanics associations, and, of course, booksellers. Books by Shaw were in the hands of such men at the beginning of careers that for some led elsewhere. The Hoyts of Deerfield, Massachusetts, passed their copy of *Civil Architecture* from generation to generation of builders. One signer, surveyor John Wheeler of Indiana, was killed at Gettysburg; Charles Bellamy apprenticed to an architect in Boston but eventually served in the Maine legislature; the Marquand Library at Princeton owns a copy of *Rural Architecture* inscribed by Jared Buell of Guilford, Connecticut, where there still stands the eponymous house he, a joiner, and William E. Weld, master-builder, erected in 1850. William F. Durfee is credited with producing the first Bessemer steel rails in this country. Thomas Van Reyper designed and built an Italianate mansion at Montclair, New Jersey, in 1872 that is now listed on the National Register of Historic Places. He was obviously so proud of his first edition of *The Modern Architect* that he had his name gold-stamped on the front cover beneath the gilt image that repeats the volume's frontispiece (see Fig. 31).[99]

These and other evidential pointers to the history and distribution of the architectural book in nineteenth-century America will be found in the following catalogue. But, unfortunately, much historical evidence has been lost when copies of books have been rebound, which may or may not have been necessary for their preservation, or inscriptions have been erased. The latter is apparently the fault of collectors and librarians who prefer a spruced-up copy, as do, of course, some antiquarian book dealers, but the process does the historian ill service, for it obliterates the evidence of a book's provenance. It wrenches the volume out of its historical context.

Shaw began his career as a mechanic with presumably just a basic common school education, so what most impresses the modern student is his referring in his books to an extraordinarily wide range of published sources compared to the books of his peers (see Appendix). He, like them, produced works as a "compiler" of information from various previous publications, many certainly known to him from secondary sources, but the sheer number of his references, acknowledged or not, sets him apart from his colleagues, although his research probably did not equal the "vast avenues of knowledge" of Thomas Ustick Walter.[100] We have earlier noted Shaw crediting the help of better educated friends in his texts. Although Shaw often mentions his sources, in many cases he does not. Intellectual property rights were not sharply defined in that era of no international copyright laws. In all of Shaw's works there are only a few recognizable footnotes citing specific sources, yet the online catalogue of Hartford's Trinity College library, for example, lists, for its copy of the 1836 edition of *Civil Architecture*, ten passages that are quotes or near quotes of earlier works. Some are old saws, some common enough, some are instructions in geometry or glossary definitions that permit of little variation. Among the variety of books cited by the Trinity catalogue are, for example, John Nicholson's *The Operative Mechanic* (1825); Joseph Gwilt, *Rudiments of Architecture* (1826); *The Works of Alexander Pope* (1822); and Archibald Alison, *Essays on . . . Taste* (1790). One such borrowing is Shaw's description of extracting lead from ore, which is "put into a reverbatory [*sic*; reverberatory] furnace, to be *roasted*," misquoted from Nicholson. The Trinity library notes five books prior to Shaw's that use the same passage. Dell Upton reports that large sections of John Haviland's *The Builder's Assistant* appear verbatim in *Civil Architecture*, as do passages from Chambers's *Civil Architecture*.[101] The present study stumbled upon four other instances of Shaw quoting verbatim, unacknowledged, an earlier work. In *Civil Architecture*, for example, his remarks on coloring marble come directly from *The Cyclopaedia; or, Universal Dictionary of Arts* (1819), and his discussion of Jeremy Bentham he lifted from Hewson

Clarks's *Cabinet of the Arts.* In *Operative Masonry* he reproduced word for word a passage from Samuel Frederick Gray's *Operative Chemistry* (1828); in *Practical Masonry* he echoes Peter Nicholson's *Practical Masonry* (1830). He also reused designs from at least one English architectural pattern book, as will be noted below. A closer scrutiny of his texts would probably reveal many other such examples, but the sheer volume of his sources, copied or not, reflects a scholarly approach to his subject.

The number of closely spaced editions or reprints of Shaw's (and Benjamin's) books seems to suggest steady sales. The longevity in print of Shaw's is more impressive: *Civil Architecture* first appeared (in part) in 1830. Hitchcock lists nine editions or reprints to 1876, but, in fact, reprints continued to appear until 1900. Among Shaw's early competitors, Minard LaFever's works barely lasted past midcentury. The same is true of Owen Biddle's book, even with the boost given it by John Haviland, whose own publication last appeared in 1830. Even Asher Benjamin's seven titles, with eighteen printings of the *Practical House Carpenter*, for example, faded in the 1850s. Of architectural texts by other authors that appeared between 1830 and the years up to the middle of the 1850s, none rivalled Shaw's in staying power. Nor did the works of Chester Hills or William Brown that closely followed. It is odd, then, that many surveys of early pattern books have failed to pay adequate attention to Shaw's works.[102] And, when he is quoted, it is usually to support an author's thesis, not to gloss Shaw's.

As the Philadelphia publisher Henry Carey Baird wrote in the Preface to the eleventh "edition" (i.e., reprint; 1870), Shaw's *Civil Architecture* "must hold a position as one of the most popular books on the subject published in this country." Although that was a salesman's pitch, it was also to a certain extent true. Notwithstanding the fact that Shaw's plates would seem to have become increasingly dated. As his repeated designs hardly kept up with changing fashion, style, or mode of presentation, it might be expected that only his prescriptive texts on geometry and methods of construction continued to prove useful. From that perspective, the "practical" would seem, not surprising, to have outlived the "theoretical" in his work. Inventories of the few libraries of major architects of the second half of the century that have been studied show, unsurprisingly, no interest in Shaw (or Benjamin for that matter) as many of the owners were trained in Europe and turned to newly studied historical styles, new materials, and new structural techniques.[103] Still, Shaw's works did not disappear entirely from architects' libraries, as the several late reprints of *Civil Architecture* attest. Perhaps its longevity stemmed from the re-emerging classicism of the Colonial and Federal revivals of the 1870s and later. That Louis H. Gibson, an Indiana architect born in 1854, when Shaw's *The Modern Architect* first appeared, approvingly included an 1843 Shaw design in his *Beautiful Houses* of 1895 suggests as much.[104] Revivalist architects, such as Hartford's William T. Marchant and Boston's Herbert W. C. Browne, added Shaw's books to their libraries late in the century.

Maine's John Calvin Stevens owned a copy of *Rural Architecture*. And the later twentieth-century upsurge of interest in neo-classicism found Shaw an admirable—and useful—example. In the 1990s Thomas Gordon Smith had students at the School of Architecture at Notre Dame building models of Shaw's domestic designs (see Fig. 25).[105] Books produced in the nineteenth-century lacked the consistency of production achieved by later publishing. What follows is an annotated catalogue rather than a descriptive bibliography.[106] Although the author hopes the following glosses include some useful notes for students of the history of the book, they are aimed primarily at the architectural historian. Entries are based on inspection of all known titles in as many actual copies as possible spread across the libraries of, mostly but not exclusively, the eastern half of the country. Glosses include mention of former owners, and, wherever possible, brief profiles of a few of them. The following lists the five titles, their editions and reissues, in chronological order. This is admittedly an incomplete study of the history and character of Shaw's literary production, one intended to lay the groundwork for further research.

1. ***Civil Architecture: / or / a Complete Theoretical and Practical / System of Building. / Containing the Fundamental Rules of the Art, / in / Geometry and Mensuration: / with the Application of Those Rules to Practice. / The True Method of Drawing the Ichnography / and Stereography of Objects; / Geometrical Rules for Shadows, / also the Five Orders of Architecture: / with a Great Variety of Beautiful Examples / Selected from Vitruvius, Stuart, Chambers and Nicholson / with / Many Useful and Elegant Ornaments, / and Rules for Projecting Them.*** In Two Volumes. Vol. 1. Boston: published by Edward Shaw and William F. Stratton, in seven parts, 1830. Registered for copyright December 22, 1829. Quarto. 76 pp. and 25 pls. (for Parts I and 2, engraved by Stratton). Hitchcock 1143.

Hitchcock found two copies of this, the first appearance of Shaw's first title, but WorldCat now lists only one, that at the Boston Public Library. There are only two chapters, "Practical Geometry" and "Projection of Shadows," numbered in pencil on this copy.

William F. Stratton (1803–46), "engraver in general" and, it should be noted, joint publisher of this first printing, advertised his business at 48 Court Street in Charles W. Moore's *Boston Masonic Mirror* during October–December 1829. His ad in *Stimpson's Boston Directory* for 1832 locates him at 15 Water Street where he "will execute Maps, Charts, Bills of Exchange, Heads of Bills, Labels ... Title Pages for publication ... Coats of Arms ... and other Engraving, upon reasonable terms. Also, Copperplate Printing attended to." He is best remembered now for his 1832 "faithful" copy of Paul Revere's famed *Bloody Massacre*.

The advertisement in the book, like the title page, says the work "consists principally of extracts from Vitruvius, Stuart, Chambers, Nicholson, and others of eminence." It is submitted to the public "for their approbation, and patronage."

The *Boston Traveler* for December 25, 1829 (three days after the registry), says that "Mr. Edward Shaw, of this city, well known as a practical architect, and a gentleman of mechanical skill and research, has been *for some time* [emphasis added] engaged in the preparation of a work which it is believed will supply the blank [in useful publications on the subject; a poke at Benjamin?] . . . and prove to be the grand desideratum. It has at length been put to press, and *will be published* [italics added] in the large quarto form, in seven numbers, the whole making about 500 [*sic*] pages, suitable for binding in two [*sic*] handsome volumes." This review consists largely of quotes from the two given chapters, as does the briefer notice of February 10, 1830, in the *National Aegis*. The latter adds that there will be ninety plates, that the second part would appear in six weeks, "and others will follow in as rapid succession as the magnitude and importance of the work will admit." (The full production of the first edition—in one volume of 176 pages and 95 plates—did not appear until 1831.) The article also notes that chapter one, on "Practical Geometry," is illustrated with eight engravings by Stratton. According to an ad in the *Traveler* of March 2, 1830, "Every subscriber is considered as subscribing for the whole work, and to pay One Dollar on the delivery of each part," and each part "will be continued with an interval of from four to six weeks between them." Agents are listed in Boston; Portland, Maine; New York; and Baltimore. The *Boston Recorder and Religious Telegraph* noted as early as January 6, 1830, that the work "is intended to comprise the mathematical and pictorial rules of Architecture forming in itself a complete treatise." "Mathematical and pictorial rules" is an apt but unconventional way of describing Shaw's approach, and perhaps it originated with him (see #3, below).

This introductory gathering was probably not widely distributed. It was self-published jointly by author and engraver (they are so listed under "New Books" in *The North American Review*, 1830). Hitchcock called this the "first edition," but in the advertisement in the third (1834), Shaw mentions only two earlier editions. He did not find a commercial publisher until the first edition of 1831, which may explain the partial appearance of this. It must have been assembled as a sample for subscribers to generate some advanced press coverage, and, perhaps more important, as a come-on to prospective publishers. The ambitious description of the intended work obviously overshot what was finally achieved.

2. *Civil Architecture: / a Complete Theoretical and Practical / System of Building. / Containing / The Fundamental Principals of the Art, / with / The Five Orders of Architecture. / Also a Great Variety of*

Examples. / Selected from / Vitruvius, Stuart, Chambers, and Nicholson; / with / Many Useful and Elegant Ornaments, / and Rules for Projecting Them, Boston: Lincoln & Edmands, 1831. Unnumbered (first) edition. Registered for copyright, March 8, 1831, by Luther Stevens.[107] From the copyright page: "John Cotton, printer, of the work from page 27 to page 40, and from page 77 to the end, including the Title page and Advertisement." 176 pp., 95 pls. (engraved by William F. Stratton, George W. Boynton, and G. W. Appleton). Hitchcock 1144.

The Boston publishing house of Ensign Lincoln (1779–1832) and Thomas Edmands (1805–33) was a small firm of booksellers that printed and published mainly religious texts and children's moralizing literature. Lincoln, a printer and senior partner, was a founder of the Massachusetts Bible Society.[108] The pair's ownership of the book was short lived. They advertised a "few copies remaining" in the *Boston Post* in February 1832, slightly less than a year after they obtained copyright. A copy in the Sterling Library at Yale University gives the publisher as Marsh, Capen and Lyon and omits the reference to John Cotton on the copyright page. It would seem that Marsh took over this first edition before issuing the second, registered in March 1832, a month after Lincoln & Edmands's last advertisement (see #3, below).

The author's grand design of 500 pages and two volumes promised in 1830 obviously proved too ambitious. The presentation here, including the full calf binding with SHAW'S / ARCHITECTURE on the spine as well as the letterpress, is weak compared to that of the second edition of 1832.

John Cotton's work must have been additions to the 1830 state. He had also printed the 1830 edition of Asher Benjamin's *Practical House Carpenter*.[109] John and Joseph Cotton constituted the "Cottons" in business as Cottons & Barnard, publishers and booksellers at 184 Washington Street. "This day published" and for sale at Lincoln & Edmands and Cottons & Barnard (*Boston Traveler*, April 15, 1831). Luther Stevens is listed as a copperplate printer at 18 State Street in *Stimpson's Boston Directory* for 1832. (He is also listed as the register for copyright for the 1852 edition of this title (see #11, below), and the publisher of Samuel Drake's *History . . . of Boston*, 1856.) A review (by Charles W. Moore?) appeared in the *Boston Masonic Mirror*, April 23, 1831. *Civil Architecture* was frequently advertised in papers in New England, and heavily in Baltimore and Charleston, South Carolina, through 1837.

The *Boston Commercial Gazette* for May 30, 1831, announced this edition under the title *Shaw's Civil Architecture*. The author, it reported, is a "practical mechanic, of more than twenty years standing, and may therefore be supposed, and he undoubtedly is, thoroughly master of the subject." The book is "a valuable compilation from Vitruvius, Stuart, Chambers and Nicholson, selected with much care and arranged with great system. . . . [It] is an important link in the chain of architectural education. We hope . . . [it] will not go unrewarded." The "chain of architectural education": other than the occasional tutelage given by architects such as Peter Banner or Solomon Willard in Boston, and others elsewhere, the books of Shaw and his contemporaries comprised the only "school" of architecture available in the United States until after the Civil War.

Shaw solicited a number of his Boston compatriots for endorsements. These included architect John Kutts ("This work is well-executed, and [I] give it as my opinion as the best American work as to theory or practical utility, and the author's exertions in presenting the public with this work deserves [*sic*] merit and extensive patronage."); architect Charles G. Hall, April 22, 1831 ("In answer to yours respecting the merits of your Book . . . I do with confidence recommend it to the public as . . . well qualified in every way to be useful for the purposes you have designed it."); and housewrights Salmon, Jeremiah, Theodore, and William Washburn, May 10, 1831 ("We find it such a work as should be in the hands of every practical builder, especially in country towns, it containing numerous examples of Grecian and Roman Architecture, judiciously selected from the best authors—embracing in a cheap volume all that is of material service to practical men . . . and cheerfully recommend it to . . . our brother mechanics, as a work well worthy of their patronage.") The Washburns knew Shaw from their work on his Equestrian Amphitheatre.

The same sort of endorsements appeared several times in the *Boston Post* from November 15, 1831, and in an ad for this book in Shaw's *Operative Masonry* of the next year. There were two additions: one from architect Joseph Jenkins, August 1, 1831 ("The more practical, or perhaps I should say operative parts of the work, strike me as being particularly useful; especially in country places, where the *Architect* is not at hand to furnish designs and plans."), and another by William Austin, the warden of the Massachusetts State Prison in Charlestown, and director of its prisoner-manned granite cutting and finishing operations, September 5, 1831 ("I feel it due to your obvious and persevering industry and deep research in all that relates to that elegant and useful art.")

In contrasting this title to his later *Rural Architecture* (see #8, below), Shaw characterized it as suited to the study of the mathematics of architecture . . . as well as . . . the scientific principles of practical details of carpentry, [and] the variety of foliage, flowers, and other ornamental parts of buildings, ancient and modern." Shaw's plates on foliage faintly suggest the underlying (or imposed upon) geometric structure of plants, a Platonic process of structuring decorative design as old as antiquity, that also more clearly governed the designs of such nineteenth-century authors as Owen Jones, and architects like Frank Furness and Louis Sullivan.[110] The edition also includes paragraphs on practical geometry, conic sections, ornaments, Grecian and Roman orders, the elements of building such as windows, doors, stairs, carpentry, arches, slating, plumbing, glazing, painting, and so on. Despite Joseph Jenkins's endorsement, there are no domestic, ecclesiastical, or other building designs. There are two glossaries, one architectural and one technical.

The advertisement in the book notes that "most writers on Civil Architecture have not entered into those Mathematical Principles, on which this noble art ultimately rests, and from which it derives its very existence." They consider it "merely as an art, than as a science also." But the student must begin with "the most simple elements of Mathematical knowledge. . . . On this principle is founded the superior skill of the Grecian and Roman Artists, which has yet been unrivalled. We should not content ourselves by merely drawing from their works, and then superadding [sic] the invention of our own imagination." Shaw thus begins his discourse by linking his subject to the long-held relationship between the rules of science (in particular geometry) and artistic expression, or, as noted above, mathematical and "pictorial" rules. He broadly places his text into a traditional mathematical context. By contrast, although Asher Benjamin begins, as does Shaw, with a section on Practical Geometry in his nearly contemporary sixth edition of *The American Builder's Companion; or, A System of Architecture,* in his Preface he limply refers to such mathematical problems "as are absolutely necessary to the well understanding of the subject."

The quotation from the text continues: The work is so arranged "to be useful to the student, as well as to all classes of operative Builders." The author will cite the "experience of the most judicious professors, give examples of both Grecian and Roman antiquities, give particular attention to the Theory of Shadows, and select "problems from the writings of English architect Peter Nicholson, easily available in this country." The reference is possibly to Nicholson's *Rudiments of Practical Perspective* of 1822. Instruction in ellipses and curves "will be found particularly useful in describing elliptical and Gothic arches. . . . After more than twenty years practice in the art of Building," the author has brought together "the following system in a concise, but intelligent manner; which consists of extracts from Vitruvius, Stuart, Chambers, and Nicholson, and other authors of eminence." This quartet provided material for the books of Shaw's competitors too. It should be kept in mind here and for other titles that Shaw may have quoted such material word for word from some older text.

Talbot Hamlin, who called Shaw's books "influential" and "exceedingly popular," although not registering the differences between the 1831 and 1832 editions of this title, recognized that it was "more a complete builder's and architect's handbook than are the Benjamin items; it has fewer designs and details, though more material on geometry, mensuration, and construction."[111]

Shaw turns the reader's attention to the construction of bridges (and other engineering works) with a description of the timber Warren Street Bridge in Boston. "Bridges of iron are the production of British ingenuity, exclusively," he wrote. He also includes Ithiel Town's own description of his lattice truss, with directions for applying to the patent holder for rights to use his system, as well as descriptions of John Rennie's Waterloo Bridge in London, both illustrated, and the Boston bridges by L. I. Cotting and Loammi Baldwin. Shaw mentions John Smeaton, Vignola, Palladio, Nicolaus Goldmann on the volute of the Ionic capital, Theodore Dwight, and Robert Hooke, "the greatest of all philosophical mechanics," on the equilibrium of arches. No doubt much of this is copied from secondary sources. As we know, his remarks on Jeremy Bentham, for example, are taken verbatim from Hewson Clarke's *Cabinet of the Arts.* By 1830 there were few specialized American publications on bridges, such as Thomas Pope's encyclopedic 1811 *Treatise on Bridge Architecture* and Town's own patent description of 1821 (republished 1825 and 1831), but here they appear as part of an architect's broader field of interest. Isaiah Rogers, Shaw's younger contemporary, would carry that interest into his own architectural practice.[112] In a letter to the editor of the *Charleston Courier* dated February 14, 1840, referring to Town's bridge as described here (and in later editions) in defense of the writer's own bridge patented in 1841, Albert Cottrell of Newport, Rhode Island, mentions "Shaw's treatise on Architecture, [as] a work well known and highly appreciated by practical mechanics."

The shortage of libraries holding this edition found in the survey suggests that the run was limited. One Avery Library copy bears the signature of Henry-Russell Hitchcock. SHAW'S / ARCHITECTURE is gilt-stamped on its spine. A second copy there is signed "John H. Wheeler / Fitchburg / Mass." Through the 1830s and 1840s, Wheeler was the town's surveyor of lumber, served on the committee of bridges, and long held the position of fire warden according to the *Old Records of the Town of Fitchburg.* The copy in the Royal Institute of British Architects' Library, London, was "Sold by John M. Ives, Essex Street, Salem." John Mansfield Ives (1799–1882) is listed as a retired bookseller in the U. S. Census for 1860. This copy is also signed: "Horatio Hoyt jr Deerfield Nov 24th 1867" and "Charles P. Hoyt, Deerfield Mass." A third signature, erased, is dated 1889. Horatio Hoyt (b. 1831) was a carpenter.[113] This work must have been passed down through the generations of one family before being shipped abroad. The copy in the library at Winterthur has laid-in an unsigned, freehand drawing of a Doric temple front, a surprisingly rare sketch found among copies examined for this study.

3. *Civil Architecture*, etc. Second Edition: Revised and Enlarged. By Edward Shaw, Architect. Boston: Published by Marsh, Capen & Lyon, no date on title page; registered for copyright, March 1832, by the publisher. Quarto. 201 pp., 97 pls. engraved by William F. Stratton, George W. Boynton, and G. W. Appleton. With "Rules of Work Originally Adopted by the Carpenters of the Town of Boston, in 1774, etc." bound in at the rear. Hitchcock 1145,

who omits the included "Rules of Work," but notes that Pl. 41 of the previous edition is omitted, and Pls. 44, 55, and 74 are new.

The Lincoln & Edmands's 1831 edition had been out for only about a year when this second edition appeared as a much improved example of bookmaking (see #2, above). Shaw's new publisher, who took over the title while it was still in its 1831 guise, was the more imposing Boston house of Marsh, Capen & Lyon (1830–ca. 1838), booksellers and producers of anthologies, histories, works on phrenology (Johann Spurzheim's among those of other authors), and Hawthorne's first book. The firm was composed of Bela Marsh, Nahum Capen, and G. Parker Lyon.[114] All of the principals were writers as well as publishers; Marsh was a member of the Massachusetts Charitable Mechanics' Association. They also published Shaw's *Operative Masonry* during this year (see #4, below). George W. Boynton was one of the leading engravers in the city. He also executed the plates for Asher Benjamin's *Builder's Guide* of 1839. George Washington Appleton, portrait painter and engraver, died age 26 in September 1831.

The new publishers produced a book that improved the presentation of the earlier edition with cloth covers using leather spine and corners. SHAW'S / ARCHITECT appears on the spine. The 1831 text was reset and better articulated, with shorter paragraphs and some new subheadings that make it easier to read than the weak typography, run-on paragraphs, and difficult-to-find headings of the earlier edition. The text here, from page 87 onward (definition of the Grecian orders), is redesigned to include a short introduction for each section cast in smaller type and set in square brackets. This bracketed text is often a paragraph or one part of a paragraph that was in the body of the text in the 1831 edition. (The sixth edition of 1852 would "enlarge and improve" on this title. See #11, below.)

The Harvard copy was presented to the library by the publishers on August 7, 1832. The book was for sale at E. L. Carey & A. Hart, Philadelphia, by August 22 (*Poulson's American Daily Advertiser*). William Lloyd Garrison's *Liberator* for October 13, 1832, reported that *Shaw's Architecture* "appears to be just such a book as was wanted by the Carpenter.... The complier has made rich and important selections from the best works." As noted earlier, the author's advertisement in this edition, dated May 1832, acknowledges "the assistance rendered by Charles W. Moore, Esq., who, has, by his judicious suggestions, and additions to the Introduction and Text, essentially promoted the improvement of the work."

Shaw's text in general divides the subject into its traditionally organized parts: the "theoretical and practical," or head-work and hand-work, a division as least as old as the ancients, and in the more recent literature such as, say, Cesare Ripa's *Iconologia* of 1593. The first, theoretical, part of Shaw's Introduction is a quick survey of the history of architecture, from "rudeness to refinement." His text sweeps, with occasional examples, from prehistory to modern English Gothic. There is minute treatment of the five classical orders, and he includes a discussion of the origin and characteristics of "the Gothic mode of building." He mentions a variety of sources: Nicholson (in the second sentence of his text); Palladio; Cato; "Rivett" (that is, Nicholas Revett); John Wood; Henry Aldrich's *Elements of Civil Architecture* as translated by the Rev. P. Smyth (2d ed. 1818); Charles Frederick Partington's *The Builder's Complete Guide* of 1825 (which Shaw must have thumbed often); James Hall's dissertation on the Gothic published in the *Transactions of the Royal Society of Edinburgh*; T. B. Armstrong's *Journal of Travels in the Seat of War, During the Last two Campaigns of Russia and Turkey,* 1831; Diodorus Siculus on the buildings of Palestine; as well as Pliny; Genesis; Theodore Dwight's *Journal of a Tour in Italy in the Year 1821;* and lines from "Liberty," an eighteenth-century poem by James Thomson lyrically characterizing the Greek orders. Some of this is found in the previous edition but some is new here. Charles W. Moore would appear to have been a man of broad learning so he would presumably have been useful in supplying such literary references as well as others found later in the text, or, perhaps, even Shaw's use of the traditional organization into the theoretical and the practical.

But other subjects discussed in this edition can hardly have been the result of Moore. In the second part of his Introduction, Shaw turns to the "practical branch of the science." "General Observations on the Construction of Houses" includes directions on siting, planning, doors and windows, how to draw a column, "mouldings," and volutes. Dispersed plates show interior doors (including "sliding doors"), front doors, partitions, a shopfront, a Doric portico, chimneypieces, but there are no complete building designs of the kind favored by Benjamin and others.

The next section is given over to the mathematical basis of architecture, to "practical" or "descriptive" geometry, illustrated with Stratton's plates, and ends with the projection of prisms and calculation of shadows. A section on foliage patterns, with plates by Boynton, precedes a description of the Greek and Roman orders with examples taken from Vitruvius; Palladio; Claude Perrault's *Ordonnance des cinq espèces de colonnes* (thus cited in a rare footnote); Vignola; Inigo Jones; Le Clerc, Chambers; Scamozzi; Bryan Higgins on masonry, whom he cites again in his contemporary *Operative Masonry*; and (perhaps owing to Charles W. Moore's influence) the ancients Tarchesius, Pytheus, and Hermogenes. Some of this was available in anthologies. There are details of buildings incorporating the various orders, but as indicated, no complete building designs.

Shaw's comments on shadows, his rules for the "projection" of prisms, and his notes on "the effect of distance of the color or objects" (what is often called *aerial perspective*) are perhaps the most important artistic aspects of his book when it was new. They were not new in the literature in general, but seem to have been new to the field of American architectural publication. (Charles Davies's *A Treatise on Shades and Shadows and Linear Perspective* of 1832, the work of a West Point mathematician, was not aimed primarily at architects, builders, or artists.) It is here that the description of Shaw's "mathematical and pictorial rules" is best supplied (see #1, above). The use of perspective presentations in this country, despite the example given by Benjamin Henry Latrobe's drawings, was rare until after the first third of the century.[115] One can trace the discussion of the practice in architectural books as far back as Vignola and beyond, but Shaw may have had access to something like Joseph Gwilt's *Sciography* (1822), "something like" because a cursory comparison of the books suggests that he did not copy anything verbatim from the Englishman (although he surely agreed with Gwilt that "He is a sorry architect who is a bad mathematician."). Another progenitor is Nicholson's *Rudiments of Practical Perspective*, already mentioned, in which Shaw could have found a chapter on the "representation of shadows," but no justification for their use.

The casting of shadows, Shaw wrote, "is one of the most interesting branches of architectural science; or perhaps it may . . . be termed branch of geometry, for it is almost entirely dependent on, and governed by, geometrical principles. From a knowledge of projection and shadows," he continued, "the architect is enabled to draft his plans, and to give to them their true effect, or representation of light and shade. . . . *The art of keeping a proper gradation of light and shade on objects, according to their several distances, colors, and other circumstances, is of the utmost consequence to the artist."* (His emphasis.) In the second part of his Introduction Shaw also wrote that "no building can ever appear to the eye in the precise form of a geometrical elevation upon paper, and as it requires considerable skill and practice to be able, from such an elevation, to form a judgment of the appearance of the edifice when actually erected, it is most satisfactory, and indeed, but just to the proprietor, to furnish him with views of the intended structure from different points of sight, accompanied by its attendant outbuildings, shrubbery, &c. such as they may be expected when brought to perfection."[116] (As late as 1843, in his Preface to *Elements of Architecture*, Benjamin's brief note mentions only a "regular set of drawings" by which "the architect is enabled to explain all parts of the building to the proprietor.")

As mentioned above, the use of perspective views of projected designs was in its infancy in this country, and, whether or not his urging had anything to do with their more frequent appearance after 1830, there is no evidence that Shaw ever made use of his own instruction. What presentation drawings we have from his hand for building projects, realized or not, show the usual orthographic plans, elevations, and details. There are some designs shown in perspective in *Rural Architecture* that were repeated in *The Modern Architect*, but they are all unshaded outlines with no representation of ambience. The one view of a realized building, the David Sears II house first published in 1843, like all of Shaw's published designs, falls far short of his written instruction (see Fig. 10). He retained his discussion in later editions of *Civil Architecture* but omitted it in his other architectural works. Perhaps he saw no need for it there because the use of perspective renderings by architects had become more common before midcentury.

To illustrate his opinions about the design of chimneypieces in which, Shaw says, "in many places the wildest notions have been indulged," he names those to be found in Isaiah Roger's Tremont House, although his own designs are not copies of them.

Recent conservationists and preservationists have dipped into Shaw's texts. Maureen Ogle points out that here his remarks on plumbing focus on tools and materials rather than what they are used for.[117] (Shaw himself cites an article on plumbing in the *Gentleman's Magazine*.) Some preservationist find much to learn from this author,[118] but Rudy Christian reports that a group of specialists found that Shaw's directions for constructing a timber frame "could not be used to create the layout." According to Christian his powers of description in this case "fall short of accuracy."

This edition was advertised in the *New York Evening Post* in January 1835. As was often the case with Shaw's titles, it was offered in tandem with works by Benjamin and LaFever. The copy of this popular edition at the Avery Library, Columbia University, came in 1953 with the Frederic Bancroft Bequest. It has SHAW'S / ARCHITECTURE embossed on the spine and is signed "Jirch [*sic*] L. Ferguson / New Bedford [Mass.] Dec 1st 1832." Jirch Ferguson is listed as a housewright in the *New-Bedford Directory* of 1838 and 1849. A copy in the Sawyer Library, Williams College, is inscribed "Thomas Marshall / Lowell [Mass.] Dec the 17-1832. Price $7.00." Marshall is listed as a housewright in the *Lowell Directory* for 1834. The copy at Northwestern University is signed on the title page by "C. B. Johnson Hartford," perhaps the Charles Buck Johnson born in that city in1819, who spent some time in Texas between homes in Little Rock, Arkansas, where he died in 1870 after a notable mercantile career. It is also signed "J. Bridges [Jnr?]." Another copy, on the market (AbeBooks) in 2014, is signed "Gridley F. Hersey, Hingham MA 1833." Hersey was a carpenter and farmer according to the local historical society. He also owned a copy of Shaw's *Operative Masonry* (see #4, below). The copy at the Canadian Centre for Architecture is signed "Samuel B. Myers Fayetteville April 21 / 1833." The copy at the Boston Athenaeum is inscribed "Henry L. [?]fish Sandwich;" that in the Rubenstein Library at Duke is signed "H. White." The copy in the Library Company of Philadelphia bears the label of Franklin Dunbar of Taunton, Massachusetts, a bookseller who died in 1834.

A copy of this edition owned by a private collector in Maine is inscribed "Hon. Charles G. Bellamy, Bought at Boston, Mass., in October, 1834. Price $7.50 while he was a student with Professor John Kurtze [i.e., Kutts] the celebrated Architect and a Dane, from Denmark in Europe—west of Russia, and south of

Norway and Sweden." (Kutts, as we have seen, had endorsed this edition.) Charles Gerrish Bellamy (1811–92) of Kittery, Maine, became a carpenter and bridge builder after "training in civil architecture and practical carpentry," obviously with the help of Shaw's tome.[119] He eventually became a justice of the peace, served in the Maine House (1842–43) and Senate (1846–47), and then took the job of Inspector of Timber at the U.S. Navy Yard in Portsmouth, New Hampshire, opposite Kittery, Maine. Given the late date at which he inscribed the book with his "Honorable" honorific, he seems to have been proud of his architectural background well into middle life.

The volume in the Hay Library, Brown University, is signed "Nathaniel Nathaniel [sic] Mowry / Smithfield / Rhode Island" and stamped "WM. G. R. MOWRY." It is also stamped "PROPERTY OF / THE ESTATE OF THE LATE / Wm. T. Nicholson." The first two owners, (Major?) Nathaniel Mowry (1774–1843) and his son, William Gulley Randall Mowry (1810–92), were members of a family long resident in Rhode Island. William trained and worked as a builder in the 1820s and 1830s, then established the lumber and building firm of Mowry & Steele in Providence. In 1856 the firm erected Mowry's house on Smith Hill there. In the 1870s Mowry served on the Board of Commissioners for the City Hall. William T. Nicholson (1834–93), founder of the Nicholson File Company in Providence, acquired the Mowry house and remodeled it twice, in 1867 and 1877. It is now known as the Mowry–Nicholson house and is listed on the National Register of Historic Places. Nicholson was inducted into the Rhode Island Heritage Hall of Fame in 2004.

The copy at the Sloane Art Library at the University of North Carolina has a number of drawings on tipped-in sheets. One is copied from Pl. 38, Fig. 1, an example of the Grecian Doric from the Temple of Thesus in Athens. It is labeled, in what looks like a learner's block lettering, DRAWN BY / MERRITT SANDS. Another sheet contains a version of the lower chimneypiece in Pl. 70, whereas others are covered with ornamental geometric drawings related to Pl. 74. These graphics also appear to be by an unskilled draftsman. One Merritt Sands of Mamaroneck, New York, born in 1842, is listed as a carpenter in the 1870 U. S. Census and as a builder in that of 1880. The title page of the copy at the Providence Public Library bears the stamp of the Providence Association of Mechanics and Manufacturers. That association's collection was transferred to the library in the 1870s.

The first free leaf of what appears to be this edition (it is missing front matter) in the collection of architect Herbert W. C. Browne (1860–1946), a European-educated, leading Neo-Colonialist of Boston, and now at Historic New England, is signed in pencil "Hiram G. Phillips / Hartford Conn. / 1874." Phillips is listed as a carpenter in *Greer's Hartford City Directory* for 1873. At Shaw's comment that none of the continental nations have "ever excelled in compositions of chimney pieces," there is a note, written perhaps by Phillips or more likely by an incredulous Browne: "What was he thinking of?" A few sketches also appear.

> 4. *Operative Masonry: / or, / A Theoretical and Practical / Treatise of Building; / Containing / a Scientific Account of Stones, Clays, Bricks, Mortars, / Cements, &c.; a Description of Their Component / Parts, with the Manner of Preparing / and Using Them. / The Fundamental Rules in Geometry, / on / Masonry and Stone-Cutting, / with their Application to Practice.* Illustrated with Forty Copper-Plate Engravings. By Edward Shaw, Architect, Author of Civil Architecture, &c., Boston: Marsh, Capen & Lyon, 1832. Registered for copyright, 1832. Octavo. 140 pp., 40 pls. Some engravings signed G. Boynton. Includes endorsements dated 1831. With "Rules for Measuring Hammered Granite adopted April 1829." Hitchcock 1159, without mention of the "Rules for Measuring."

The ampersand after "Civil Architecture" represents a fabrication. No other known Shaw titles exist this early. The *Boston Post* noted this work as just published on April 26, 1832, a month or so after the appearance of the second edition of *Civil Architecture*, also published by Marsh, Capen & Lyon (see #3, above) (Fig. 21). This appeared in a plain green cloth binding with paper label on the spine: SHAW'S / OPERATIVE / MASONRY. Shaw's *Practical Masonry* of 1846 (see #9, below) is a somewhat altered version of this work.

According to John Bryan, this was "the most comprehensive treatment of masonry by an American when it was published."[120] Judging by Hitchcock's bibliography, when published it was the only such work to have appeared in this country (Minard Lafever's *Modern Builder's Guide* of 1833 does contain a section on masonry.) In England in 1827 Peter Nicholson issued *Popular and Practical Treatise on Masonry and Stonecutting* and, in 1830, *Practical Masonry, Bricklaying, and Plastering*. Neither of these appears to have been cited here, although one or the other probably inspired this one. Shaw is named among the signatories to the 1829 "Rules for Measuring Hammered Granite" bound herein.

Under the title *Shaw's Operative Masonry*, the *Boston Traveler* for June 26, 1832, after mentioning the author as "the gentleman who was so successful a year or two since in compiling a large work on architecture," describes this as "a less voluminous treatise . . . which is presented to his mechanical friends in the best typographical style of Messrs March, Capen and Lyon."

From the Preface: The "Compiler" (a word repeated twice again) notes that since permanency in building seems more desirable than formerly, "it has been thought that a brief account of the nature and qualities of [masonry] building materials, with a short exposition of their component parts, would not be misplaced in a treatise of this kind. . . . The best writers, on the various subjects treated of in this book, have been consulted, and such use made of their labors, by abridging,

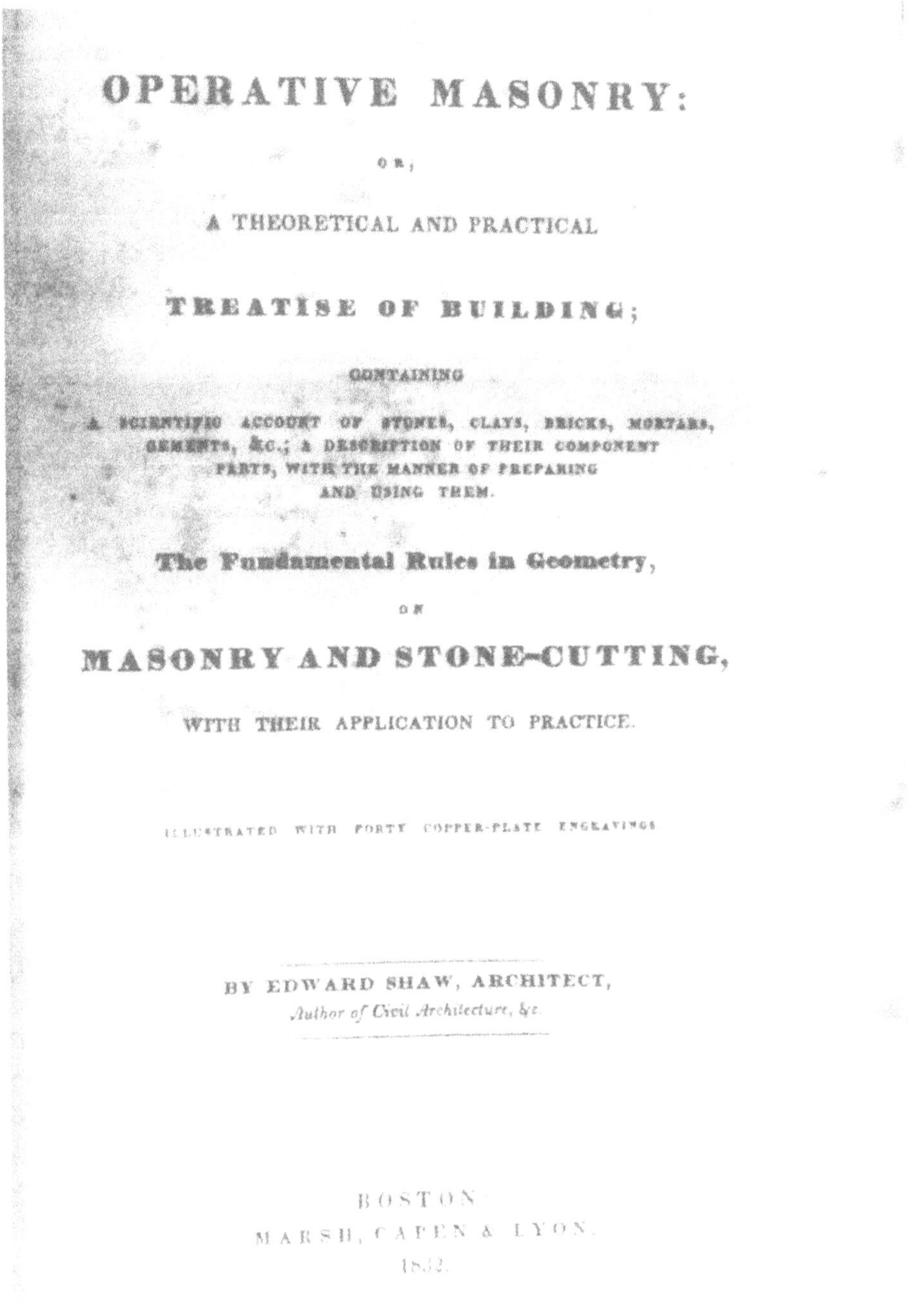

OPERATIVE MASONRY:

OR,

A THEORETICAL AND PRACTICAL

TREATISE OF BUILDING;

CONTAINING

A SCIENTIFIC ACCOUNT OF STONES, CLAYS, BRICKS, MORTARS,
CEMENTS, &c.; A DESCRIPTION OF THEIR COMPONENT
PARTS, WITH THE MANNER OF PREPARING
AND USING THEM.

The Fundamental Rules in Geometry,

ON

MASONRY AND STONE-CUTTING,

WITH THEIR APPLICATION TO PRACTICE.

ILLUSTRATED WITH FORTY COPPER-PLATE ENGRAVINGS

BY EDWARD SHAW, ARCHITECT,

Author of Civil Architecture, &c.

BOSTON

MARSH, CAPEN & LYON.

1832.

Figure 21　Edward Shaw, title page to *Operative Masonry*, Boston: Marsh, Capen & Lyon, 1832.
Author's collection.

altering, abstracting, and condensing, as seemed advisable to the Compiler. While he has added much that has been the result of many years of practical experience and personal observation," his aim has been "brevity with perspicuity, and utility with cheapness."

There is but one "architectural" illustration, that of the Doric column. This is not just a builder's how-to manual but, in addition, an almost scholarly *omnium-gatherum* on various materials, including their chemical compositions, European and American sources, and methods of masonry construction from antiquity to the present. Because it is highly unlikely that he travelled abroad, Shaw needed to compile his information from his wide bookish research (see Appendix). His many references to scientific publications was unequaled by his peers. On the subject of mortar, for example, his gleanings include those from Pliny; Vitruvius; James Hall's studies on granite published in the *Transactions of the Royal Society of Edinburgh*; (probably) the second volume of Robert Doffie's *Memoirs of Agriculture* of 1771; A. J. Loriot, *Mémoire sur une découverte dans l'art de batir*, 1774 (English translation, 1775); Bryan Higgins, a British chemist who in 1780 published *Experiments . . . Made with the View of Improving . . . Calcareous Cements*. Shaw also refers to the works of Alberto Fortis; a German chemist he names "Vauquebin" (i.e., Louis Nicolas Vauquelin); the Athenian marble brought to Paris by Charles-Marie-Francois Olier, the marquis de Nointel; Martin Heinrich Klaproth on mica; the English geologist White Watson; what seems to be a reference to the Swede Torbern Olof Bergman (although Shaw wrote "Bergaman" without the given names); quotes an excerpt from the patent awarded John Cartwright, an English brick maker, in the 1790s; and Benjamin Thompson, Count Rumford. He silently reproduces verbatim the description of the discovery of the process of coloring marble by Athanasius Kircher and Albert Gunter in Samuel Frederick Gray's *The Operative Chemist* of 1828, a book he referred to often. His text describes various types of foreign and domestic stone, their chemical composition, and their uses, with examples, such as a table in the Hotel de la Monnie at Paris made of Leek Marble (*marbe poireau*).

Shaw here provided an apt treatise on the materials and building methods worthy of Boston's current neoclassical era. He mentions several Boston Granite Style buildings, including the large "piers" of Boston's (Faneuil Hall) "Market-House," Tremont House, Tremont Theatre, the United States Bank; the sienite at the unfinished Bunker Hill monument and "Washington Bank"; and the sandstone of St. Paul's Church in Boston as well as the federal Capitol.

But the bulk of the book is devoted to illustrated geometrical problems of which the heading of Section V will give an inkling: CONSTRUCTION OF THE MOULDS FOR HORIZONTAL CYLINDRETIC VAULTS, EITHER TERMINATING RIGHTLY OR OBLIQUELY, UPON PLANE OR CYLINDRICAL WALLS, WITH THE JOINTS OF THE COURSES EITHER IN THE DIRECTION OF

THE VAULT, PERPENDICULAR TO THE FACES, OR IN SPIRAL COURSES.
Section XVI concerns stones used in Gothic arches and vaults. Later sections
cover brick construction, the construction of chimneys, and the design of fireplaces
and chimneypieces.

An unsigned review of *Operative Masonry* in Charles W. Moore's *Boston
Masonic Mirror*, May 12, 1832, echoes the Preface by lamenting the flimsy wooden
architecture of the country erected in "perishable materials" and thus, in the
spirit of improvement, hands this book "a hearty welcome. While the author
gives a clear and lucid account of the best materials and modes of using them,
all useless and well known subjects are avoided. . . . Not only should our wealthy
fellow-citizens in the country, as well as in town, turn their attention to more
durable materials . . . but they would do well to inquire if science in planning,
and elegance of execution, may not very properly be encouraged."[121] In *The
Modern Architect*, Shaw (or "The Editors"?) wrote that "If this science were more
generally studied throughout the United States, we should be exempt from those
architectural abortions which now so often disgrace our cities and villages" (see
#12, below). That statement seems to echo Moore's.

The chronological and rhetorical parallels between Shaw's works on masonry
construction and Charles W. Moore's on the fraternal order of Freemasonry are
intriguing. The publication date here coincides with that of the second edition
of *Civil Architecture* (see #3, above), also published by Marsh, Capen & Lyon,
in which, as we have seen, Shaw acknowledges the assistance of Moore, a Masonic
leader active in the Boston Mechanics Institution (see Chapter 1). Given that
Shaw was looking for help from Moore on the text of *Civil Architecture*, we would
not be amiss in attributing to him some influence on this book as well. Although
Shaw produced a rejected design for the Boston Masonic Temple in 1830, no
evidence has been uncovered that he was a member of the Masonic brotherhood.
Nonetheless, the Freemasons' use of architectural imagery is well known. *The
Masonic Trestle-Board* published by Moore in 1843 includes the following: "By
operative masonry, we allude to a proper application of the useful rules of
architecture, whence a structure will derive figure, strength, and beauty [certainly
a reference to Vitruvius], and whence will result a due proportion and just
correspondence in all its parts. It furnishes us with dwellings, and convenient
shelters from the vicissitudes and inclemencies [*sic*] of the seasons; and while
it displays the effects of human wisdom, as well in the choice as in the arrangement
of the sundry materials of which an edifice is composed, it demonstrates that a
fund of science and industry is implanted in man, for the best, most salutary,
and beneficial purposes." There follows a discussion of the five orders of classical
architecture. Did Shaw teach Moore the orders, or did Moore expand their meaning
for him?

Harvard's copy was a gift of the publishers on August 7, 1832. The *New York
Post* ran an ad for this work in May 1834. The copy at the University of Virginia

is signed "John M. Dodd's / Book / May 7th 1832 / New York / $5" (just days before Moore's review appeared), as well as "9-24-61 Theo. Thiele" and "Lydia F. Washburn." It also has Paul Mellon's bookplate. Dodd (ca. 1805–88) appeared in the Manhattan newspapers as a mason who was a director (1834) and president (1839) of the Mechanics Institute (not to be confused with The General Society of Mechanics & Tradesmen of which he was also a member, and, as we shall see, also had copies of Shaw's books), and as a builder in 1860. A Theodore Thiele of New York enlisted in the Union army on October 30, 1861, just five weeks after his presumed signature appears in this book.[122] The copy now at the Getty Research Institute came from the Franklin Institute in Philadelphia. The copy at the Sawyer Library, Williams College, is signed "Augustine Burt." A man of that name (1810–81) of Springfield, Massachusetts, was, among other things, a bookseller according to the 1870 U.S. Census and city directories. The copy in the Marquand Library at Princeton bears the name of A. L. Bayly; that in the library at Notre Dame is signed "The Property of J. F. P. Hunt." The copy on the market in 2015 from Braintree Used Books is signed Gridley F. Hersey, Hingham (Mass) 1833. Hersey also owned the 1832 edition of *Civil Architecture* (see #3, above). The title page of the copy at the Providence Public Library bears the stamp of the Providence Association of Mechanics and Manufacturers. That association's collection came to the library in the 1870s.

Charles Q. Clapp donated a copy of "Shaw on Masonry " among other books on architecture to the Maine Charitable Mechanic Association in Portland according to the *Eastern Argus* of March 30, 1838. That could only have been *Operative Masonry,* a book the Association transferred to the American Antiquarian Society in 1930. Clapp (1799–1869) was remembered at his death as possessed of "an unusual taste for architecture." He was, in fact, a real estate developer, "an astute businessman who used his architectural skills to improve his commercial properties." His major surviving work is his own brick house, Roman in form but Grecian in detail, the erection of which coincided with the publication of *Operative Masonry.* The house still stands on Spring Street, now part of the Portland Museum of Art and listed on the National Register of Historic Places.[123]

The copy of this title in the Kroch Library at Cornell University is signed on the first free page "Wm F. Durfee Book" and "Wm F. Durfee / New Bedford Mass / 1856." It was the gift of the (Henry W.) Sage Endowment Fund in 1891. William Franklin Durfee (1833–99) began his professional life as an architect and civil engineer trained at the Lawrence School at Harvard. He worked in New Bedford, Massachusetts, after graduation, designed and directed construction of the Gosnold Iron Works there, and served as a state representative, all before 1862. In that year he was charged with designing, overseeing construction of, and operating an experimental steel works at Wyandotte, Michigan. There he directed the production of the first Bessemer steel rails manufactured in this country. He went on to other creative work, such as producing the steel used in the pioneering Eads Bridge across the Mississippi River at St. Louis. He was elected to all the prestigious societies in the field of civil engineering, and died full of honors.[124]

One Avery Library copy is signed "Wm Jening or Jenny [?] / New York Dec 1857," and there are plans sketched inside the back cover; another, with SHAW'S / OPERATIVE / MASONRY on the spine, has the signature of William Babbet. The copy in the Library Company of Philadelphia is signed by both John and William W. Torbert. William added "Wilmington, Delaware," and "January 25, 1836." John Torbert (1775–1842) was a banker also involved in the milling industry. His son, William Warner Torbert (1812–83), was also a banker perhaps also involved in the milling industry. There is a pencil drawing of a stone archway on the rear flyleaf. In the Torbert–Ellegood papers in Special Collections at the University of Delaware, series III, F16, there is a volume of "tables, drawings, and engineering notes" from 1835 associated with William. A copy was donated to the American Antiquarian Society in 1930 by the Worcester County Mechanics Association, founded in 1842. The book was for sale in Boonville, Missouri, in August 1845 (*Boon's Lick Times*). The Boston Public Library copy was the gift of Mrs. F. B. Green, December 28, 1897. The title page of the copy in the Hay Library is stamped BROWN / UNIVERSITY.

The copy listed in catalogue 165 (2015) of bookseller Charles B. Wood III is inscribed "Thomas Ditson." That at the University of Delaware is signed on the verso of Pl. 40 "Mrs. M. N. Nast." The copy in the library at Dartmouth came from the College's Thayer School of Civil Engineering, given by General Sylvanus Thayer, the "father of West Point." (His 1867 donation was intended for a "School or Department of Architecture or Civil Engineering." MIT opened the first school of architecture in this country in that year.) The copy in the Davis Library at the University of North Carolina is signed Wm. Beverhart[?] Thompson. There are a few reader's additions and corrections throughout the text. The copy at the Canadian Centre for Architecture is inscribed "For the Wayland [Massachusetts] Town / Library / From—Geo. Hayward / Boston / July 1857." There is also a Wayland library plate. A George W. Hayward appears in Boston city directories in the 1850s as a "daguerrean artist." The copy in the St. Louis Mercantile Library is stamped "War Department Library" as well as "Association of American Railroads."

5. *Civil Architecture*, etc. Third Edition, Revised and Enlarged. Boston: Marsh, Capen & Lyon, 1834. Registered for copyright, 1834. Advertisement dated Dec. 1833. Quarto. 208 pp., 100 pls. by William F. Stratton and George W. Boynton. Hitchcock 1146.

Examples of this edition appear in full calf with SHAW'S / ARCHITECT in gold on the spine. The truncated second word of the title stems from the fact that here (and in other examples) ACHITECTURE would not fit horizontally on the width of the spine.

Hearty sales must have prompted this quick, minor revision of the 1832 edition. The advertisement states that three new plates (64 [designs for imposts], 71, and 72 [designs for cornices]) have been added, and that the author asserts that he "feels confident it comprises as great a variety of useful matter as can be produced for the price at which it is afforded; and he has not . . . filled this work with useless pictures, and essays of unmeaning matter, more for show than utility." It is submitted to "an enlightened public, after tendering his sincere thanks for their very liberal patronage of the two [sic] former editions, hoping to receive a share that may be due in this." This sounds like a dig at his competitors. Benjamin, Haviland, and Lafever had all produced books in the previous year. His addressing "an enlightened public" rather than mechanics is noteworthy.

Advertised for sale, *New York Evening Post*, May 26, 1834, and "by the quantity or single" in the *Post* for January 21, 1835. A copy signed "Americus V. Parker's Property, Belfast [Maine] Septr 22 1834 $6.00" (followed by a Greek inscription) was on the market in 2015 at DeWolfe and Wood, Alfred, Maine. Americus V. Parker, Esq., then of Waldo, Maine, married in 1848. In 1998 Ross Levett Antiques, Thomaston, Maine, had a copy of this edition signed by "M. R. Hanson [or Hansen] / Palmyra Me." The Walter Havighurst Collection in the library at Miami University of Ohio has a well-used, not to say abused, copy with a series of signatures. The oldest appears to be that of Charles Lecompt (although the surname as written seems to be Leompt) who dated it at Springfield (Ohio?) September 18, 1852. The names R. E. Horstman or Richard Horstman appear three times. Once from Indianapolis, undated, once without location dated "Sept 2nd 1889," and once from Springfield, Ohio, dated "Dec 25 90." The copy in the Phillips Library of the Peabody Essex Museum is stamped JAMES H. BALLOU, A.I.A. / ARCHITECT / 125 DERBY ST. SALEM, MASS. Ballou's papers (1963–85) are also at the Phillips Library. Obviously this was acquired as reference for an Essex County architect and restorationist. Ballou was project architect for the renovation of the Quincy Market, Boston, in the 1970s.

6. *Civil Architecture: / or / A Complete Theoretical and Practical / System of Building. / Containing / The Fundamental Principles of the Art, / with / The Five Orders of Architecture. / Also a Great Variety of Examples. / Selected from / Vitruvius, Stuart, Chambers, and Nicholson, / with / Many Useful and Elegant Ornaments, / and Rules for Projecting Them.* Fourth Edition, Revised and Enlarged, Boston: Marsh, Capen & Lyon, 1836. Registered for copyright, 1834. Quarto. 208 pp., 100 pls. by William F. Stratton and George W. Boynton. Press of N. Southard, 9 Cornhill. Hitchcock 1147.

Again brisk sales must have prompted this quick new issue. The advertisement signed "E.S." is dated "Boston, December, 1833." In the Preface to his *Rural Architecture* of 1843, Shaw wrote that this, the fourth "edition," which he dated 1834, was the "most complete" one. It is in fact identical to the third edition, and therefore a reprint. Full calf with SHAW'S / ARCHITECT on a label on the spine. There are directions to the binder at the end of the Introduction, architectural and technical glossaries at the end of the text.

As noted above, the online catalogue of Hartford's Trinity College lists ten places in the "fourth edition" in which Shaw has reproduced passages of text from other writers. This kind of borrowing would apply to other editions as well.

For sale in Norwich, Connecticut, early in 1836 (*Norwich Courier,* January 13), and Hartford (*Patriot and Eagle,* March 18). For sale in Fredonia, New York, in June 1836.[125] Advertised in *The Madisonian* of Washington, DC, in October 1839. For sale as late as December 1845, in the *Pittsburgh Daily Post.* On February 16, 1839, Col. Valentine Darragh (?) of Cumberland County, Virginia, signed his copy of this edition. It is now at the University of Virginia. The copy at the Loeb Library of Harvard University is inscribed "The property of Richard Jenney [?] and Jefferson Cree [?]." The copy at the Firestone Library at Princeton bears the block initials "S.W. NY" (?) and "A. M. Sept 1868." The copy at the Hay Library, Brown University, has a label that reads "DONATION / OF THE / CLASS OF 1821 / TO THE / LIBRARY OF / BROWN UNIVERSITY / 1846."

A smattering of architectural books once owned by the immigrant Kentucky architect Thomas Lewinski included this edition, which is now in the library at the University of Kentucky. It was once also in the possession of the poet James Hillary Mulligan, and, in 1950, in the private library of William Combs of Lexington. Clay Lancaster suggested Pl. 74, Fig. 1, a design for a shopfront, as the inspiration for the projecting entrance bay of Lewinski's James Clay villa in Lexington, whereas the chimneypiece in Pl. 73 suggested the library mantel there. Lancaster also thought the Grecian Doric details in Pl. 37 were used on the Allen (or Craig) house near Georgetown, whereas Pl. 73, a design for a front door, was repeated at the William Leavy villa, The Elms, near Lexington.[126] The front entrance added in the 1840s to Shawnee Springs, the George C. Thompson house near Harrodsburg, Kentucky, also derives from the shopfront in this work according to the nomination form of the National Register of Historic Places.

A copy in a private collection in North Carolina is signed on the title page "James Sampson his Book" and contains his bookplate. James D. (for Drawborn) Sampson (1806–61) was a free mixed-race house carpenter in antebellum Wilmington, North Carolina, the well-to-do head of a household of builders. At his death he left several properties, including a workshop, tools, and lumber. The existing house at 602 Walnut Street in Wilmington is said to have been built in 1860 by Sampson for his own use.[127]

The copy at the Athenaeum of Philadelphia came from the Lowell (Mass.) City Library to which it had been the gift of the Rev. L. C. Manchester, long time rector of St. John's Episcopal Church there. The copy at the American Antiquarian Society is stamped W. MARTIN JONES JR. / GEO. S. RILEY 1919. One W. Martin Jones, Jr., who lived in Rochester, New York, was a member of the American Bar Association that year. George S. Riley, owner of extensive real estate within the city of Rochester, died in 1919. A copy on the market in 2015 at the William Reese Company bears the name of William T. Marchant (1880–1948), a Hartford architect, designer of the Wood Memorial Library in South Windsor, Connecticut (1926), houses in and around Hartford, and many other neo-Colonial buildings. The Connecticut Historical Society has drawings for 400 projects by him.

7. *Civil Architecture*. Fifth Edition, between 1836 and 1852; no copies known: see comment by Shaw at #11, below. Mentioned by Hitchcock under 1149.

8. *Rural Architecture: / Consisting of / Classic Dwellings, / Doric, Ionic, Corinthian and Gothic, / and / Details Connected with Each of the Orders; / Embracing / Plans, Elevations Parallel and Perspective, / Specifications, Estimates, Framing, Etc. / for / Private Houses and Churches. / Designed for the / United States of America.* By Edward Shaw, Architect. Author of Civil Architecture, Operative Masonry, etc., Boston: James B. Dow, Publisher, 1843. Registered for copyright, 1843, by Edward Shaw. William A. Hall & Co., Printers, 12 Water Street. Quarto. 108 pp., 52 plates engraved by W. W. Wilson. Hitchcock 1161.

Hitchcock mentions only 52 plates, but other copies contain 58 or 60 (as does the copy at the University of Delaware) without, however, descriptions to accompany them. They show stair details, and so on, which appear with notes in the rare second edition (see #10, below) and are repeated in *The Modern Architect* (see #12, below). "Just published" according to the *Boston Recorder*, September 14, 1843 (Fig. 22).

Shaw uses a different Boston publisher here, Marsh, Capen & Lyon having gone out of business, and a new engraver who will appear from now on (for Wilson, see Chapter 1). James Barber Dow (1807–77) was a Boston South End bookseller, stationer, and dealer in fancy goods who published religious works on the order of Harvey Newcomb's *The Young Lady's Guide to the Harmonious Development of Christian Character* (1841).

Some copies are bound in full calf with RURAL / ARCHITECTURE stamped on the spine. Others, as well as some later editions of *Civil Architecture* (Fig. 23), are handsomely cloth bound with a gold-stamped Nativity scene set amid

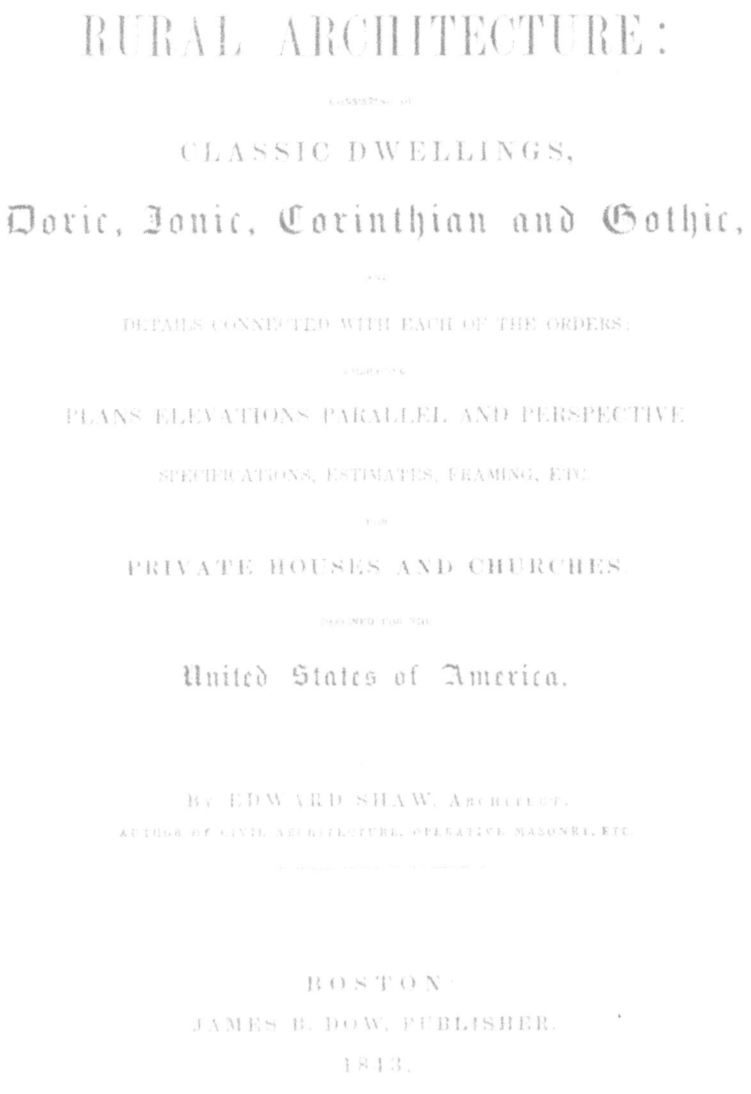

RURAL ARCHITECTURE:

CLASSIC DWELLINGS,

Doric, Jonic, Corinthian and Gothic,

DETAILS CONNECTED WITH EACH OF THE ORDERS:

PLANS ELEVATIONS PARALLEL AND PERSPECTIVE

SPECIFICATIONS, ESTIMATES, FRAMING, ETC.

PRIVATE HOUSES AND CHURCHES

United States of America.

BY EDWARD SHAW, ARCHITECT.

AUTHOR OF CIVIL ARCHITECTURE, OPERATIVE MASONRY, ETC.

BOSTON:
JAMES B. DOW, PUBLISHER.
1843.

Figure 22 Edward Shaw, title page to *Rural Architecture*, Boston: James B. Dow, 1843. Courtesy of the Lilly Library, Indiana University.

classical and medieval ruins in a mountainous landscape on the front cover, blind stamped on the back, and a spine with a gold-stamped composition of, in descending order, carpenters' tools, title, church spire, and publisher's name. The image on the front cover, having nothing to do with the content of the book, obviously came from an engraver's stock, a common enough practice at the time. In these years, book illustrations also often stood at arm's length in relation to

Figure 23   Cover of *Shaw's Civil Architecture,* 1852, with gold-stamped Nativity scene on the front cover; carpenter's tools, church tower, and spire on spine. Courtesy, American Antiquarian Society.

text. Longfellow was "bound to protest" to his publishers, for example, about illustrations to his *Poets and Poetry of Europe* (1845), which had "no connection with the subjects in the book."[128] Nonetheless, the New York-published *Merchants' Magazine and Commercial Review* for February 1, 1844, called this title "a splendid quarto, produced in a manner highly creditable to the enterprising publisher," and noted that it is "as ornamental as useful, and should be found in the library of every liberal gentleman and scholar. We know of no work better calculated to impart to or foster in the young a correct knowledge and taste for the science of architecture, and as such, we recommend it to heads of families." It seems that the author and/or publisher intended some copies for library display rather than or as well as, indoor study or on-site use, although the internal layout retained the old-fashioned look of his *Civil Architecture* when compared to the stylebooks of Shaw's younger contemporaries.

Shaw's Preface tells us how this "little Treatise" differs from his *Civil Architecture*. He recommends his earlier title to those who wish "to go into the study of the mathematics of architecture, embracing in that term the doctrine of 'lights and shadows,' as well as to enter upon the scientific principles and practical details of carpentry, and to make themselves acquainted with the variety of foliage, flowers, and other ornamental parts of buildings, ancient and modern." He now wishes to compete more closely if rather belatedly with the publications of his competitors, "to lay before the reader, and especially the practical architect, a variety of plans, elevations, &c . . . principally [of] dwelling-houses, and places of public worship." His main object will have been attained if his plans for houses and places of public worship, developed out of his thirty years as a practical builder, are found useful "in an art to which men, in a civilized state are indebted for most of the comforts, and for all the elegancies in their houses, or in those which they enter for the worship of the Most High."

The front section is divided into three parts: history, the architectural styles, and the arrangement and construction (mainly) of houses. Parts I and II, on the "History and Progress of Architecture," and "Characteristics of the Different Styles of Architecture," contain a chronological roll call of national styles, and are characteristic products of the Whig-inspired concept of history as essentially a series of improvements. In Part I, the sweep of history again begins at the beginning, as it did in *Civil Architecture,* and as it does in the works of Shaw's competitors, with Cain building the city of Enoch, but now focuses here on the development from the Italian Renaissance to the latest catalogue of English achievements. The author lists what we now call "starchitects" from Alberti to Palladio, takes a swipe at Bernini and "depraved" Borromini, then turns to England. He mentions in passing Jones, Wren, Vanbrugh, Hawksmoor, Kent, Gibbs, and Wyatt. The first section of Part II lines up the sequence of Western styles and some of their parts that then constituted the details of architectural history: Egypt, Greece and Rome, Tuscan, Doric, Ionic, Composite, and Corinthian, Persian and caryatide supports, pilasters, pedestals, pediments, (English) Gothic, Decorated, and Perpendicular. He illustrates his own residential designs based on most of these styles. Along the way Shaw adds to his earlier sources, citing a virtual library of works: William Bullock on Mexico, (Henry?) Bromley (i.e., Anthony Wilson), (John?) Mitford on James Gibbs, James Stuart (and Nicholas Revett, with Willey Revely's added volume) on Athenian architecture, Vivant Denon on Egypt, Vitruvius, Vignola, William Chambers (cited often), Edmund Aikin on the Doric order, Peter Nicholson's *Dictionary*, Scamozzi, Sebastien LeClerc, Joseph Gwilt's *Encyclopaedia*, Roland Frèart de Chambray's *Parallèle*, Francois Blondel's *Cours*, Thomas Rickman, and Pugin's ever handy *Specimens*. It is here, too, that he first published the Rev. John Pierpont's letter with his measurements of the Parthenon, a letter in which he mentions (and disagrees with) some of the figures published by the English antiquarian William Martin Leake in his *Topography of Athens* of 1821.

Despite such citing of precedent, in this work the author apparently reproduces less of the texts of others than he had for *Civil Architecture*, and we get somewhat more clearly his own voice. In the final section of Part II, "Architecture in America," the author names the latest "models . . . of the purest Grecian, or the more beautiful Gothic styles," for the design of some of which he had lost the competition but apparently bore no grudge. His selection parallels that of contemporary critics. He mentions the names of no architects: the U. S. Capitol (before Thomas U. Walter's additions) heads the list, followed by William Strickland's United States Bank in Philadelphia as well as his Merchants' Exchange and Mint, and especially Walter's Girard College, "a magnificent specimen of the Corinthian order." He overlooks works by Latrobe. In New York he singles out Town and Davis's Grecian Custom House and their building for New York University, "a beautiful specimen of the Gothic style." George Brimmer's now vanished Trinity Church in Summer Street, Boston, in "rough granite Gothic has a beautiful, massive and imposing front . . . [and] the interior excels that of any other church in our city in beauty." He cites frescoed walls, "the clusters of pillars, the oaken woodwork, and the ornamental chancel." But Shaw then notices that the central arch of the roof is "altogether out of proportion . . . and certainly adds no beauty." Richard Bond's now demolished Gore Hall, the new library for Harvard, and Isaiah Rogers's First Church across the way "are among our best specimens of Gothic." The spire of Bulfinch's now removed Federal Street church is "much to be admired." Among the Doric works he mentions A. B. Young's Custom House, Bulfinch's lost United States Branch Bank, and Alexander Parris's Quincy Market, "a plain but noble structure of hewn granite . . . constructed by, and an honor to, our city." Parris's St. Paul's ("Stone Chapel"), and Rogers's Suffolk Bank and Masonic Temple (with its "chaste and dignified" façade) are cited as examples of the Ionic order. Both have vanished. The rotunda of Rogers's demolished Merchants' Exchange represents the Corinthian style. Shaw's critical (or rather uncritical) approach was through a catalogue of stylistic details, and it must be observed that his judgments did not coincide well with other Boston critics such as Henry Cleveland or ill-tempered Arthur Gilman. The latter, for example, found Rogers's rotunda "a tawdry and miserable failure." As we shall see, he would not be kind to Shaw either.

Part III includes, among other prescriptions, a brief discussion of the proportions of spaces and their decoration, notes on the elements of houses from doors to chimneypieces and stairs, the warming of houses, designs for houses, and church architecture.

This is the first book in which Shaw discusses and illustrates designs for complete buildings: a series of houses inspired by the classical orders; the Gothic;

and other styles, including Tudor. He had available Samuel H. Brooks's *Designs for Cottage and Villa Architecture; Containing Plans, Elevations, Sections, Perspective Views and Details for the Erection of Cottages and Villas,* London: Thomas Kelly, 1839. From Brooks he took not only the general layout of his plates as stated in the extended title of the English publication: plans, elevations, sections, perspective views, and details for the erection of cottages and villas," but had William Wilson, his engraver, copy verbatim Brooks's plates IV, V, and VI. These reappear here as plates 29, 30, and 50. Shaw also appropriated Brooks's "Reference Sheet of Details" describing his plate VI, although Shaw did employ a few synonyms. It should be noted too, that our author avoided the more picturesque English domestic designs. His Grecian Ionic house, for example, is a parallelepiped set on an axially arranged, T-shaped plan (Figs. 24–25). Nonetheless, those borrowed designs were hardly intended for the United States, as the title of this edition avers.

There are also designs for Gothic churches (Figs. 26–27). In his discussion of church building, the author emphasizes iconography over stylistic details. He recognizes that, given the present state of the country, to imitate the great Gothic structures of the old world would be very difficult. "But we cannot but indulge the hope, that, ere long . . . we may yet equal them in regard to the taste and architectural simplicity of these structures; [whose] qualities [are] more in harmony with our republican form of government" than the cathedrals of York, Milan, or Rome. In considering the design of a church, remember, he wrote, that the "lofty spire, pinnacles, and finals [*sic*], seem as many fingers pointing toward the heaven. . . . In the massive tower and battlements, the mind perceives an emblem of the stability of truth, and of the gracious promises of God. . . . On entering, the mind swells with the feeling of sublimity . . . to rise in adoration of the Being." The heaven-pointing spire and such other Romantic interpretations of Gothic churches were then (and still are) oft-recurring in religious and poetical writing. Indeed, in this section Shaw quotes from Sir Walter Scott's "The Lay of the Last Minstrel" (1805).

In his well-known, forty-five page, ostensible book review occasioned by the publication of *Rural Architecture*, which appeared in the April 1844 issue of the *North American Review*, a twenty-three-year-old Arthur Gilman devoted what seems, almost as an afterthought, just the last few pages to the book and its author. Shaw is now chiefly remembered as the target of this truly vicious, ad hominem attack. The preceding text is a sweeping and generally scathing criticism of the state of American architecture in general.[129] Young Gilman was in no mood to be nice (was he ever?) when he turned his loaded cannon on Shaw. Fresh out of Trinity College, Hartford, Gilman savaged the self-educated former mechanic. That we might somewhat agree with his criticism does not make it any the easier to read: "Mr. Shaw . . . has written and published several works upon subjects connected with the profession of architecture. We have no doubt, that he can draw

PL. 25

GRECIAN IONIC

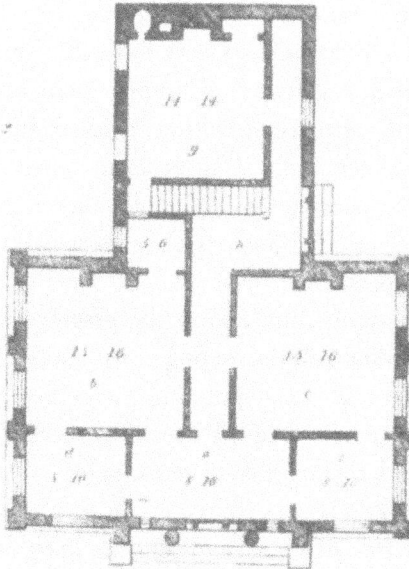

Figure 24 Edward Shaw, Grecian Ionic house, plate 25 of *Rural Architecture* (1843). Author's collection.

the contract and indite the specifications for carpenters' and masons' operations, as well as any of his professional compeers. . . . We do not see, in the work before us, any evidence of much greater ability. The author appears to be one of those old fashioned five-order men, who have grown antic in the decline of their favorite system . . . [but] it is not hard to perceive, that he has merely discarded Vitruvius for Benjamin, and Sir William Chambers' 'Treatise' for 'The Builder's Guide.'"

Figure 25 Model of Shaw's Grecian Ionic house produced by students at the School of Architecture, Notre Dame University, 1990s. Courtesy Thomas Gordon Smith.

There are plenty Doric and Corinthian houses with "faultlessly exact" details, "no doubt minutely transcribed from Stuart; but it is only the skin of the lion on the body of the ass. The parts are grouped into grotesque and heterogeneous forms, and fitted together as a child fits the pieces of a wooden puzzle." Of such a domestic design as shown in Pls. 9 and 10, Gilman wrote: "For originality in the invention of ugliness, it may stand without a parallel." His attack on Shaw is recognized as a turning point, away from antiquity toward the medieval and Italianate, in the so-called "Battle of Styles" in nineteenth-century American architecture.

From our perspective we can take criticism a step farther without the vitriol of Gilman. It should be noted that he had just favorably reviewed (twice) A. J. Downing's *Cottage Residences* (1842) in the *North American Review*.[130] Obviously Shaw's cottages could not compete with A. J. Davis's designs for Downing. In a work of the 1840s entitled *Rural Architecture*, Shaw continued primarily to empha-size isolated classical forms illustrated in copper engravings, whereas his contem-poraries, such as Davis and Downing, W. B. Lang in his publication on his cottages at Roxbury of 1845 (some reproduced in Louisa Tuthill's *History of Architecture* of 1848), or Gervase Wheeler in his *Rural Homes* of 1851, were introducing picturesque Gothic cottages in rural settings rendered in shaded lithographs or woodcuts locked within the text. Shaw's domestic "Gothic" designs

93

Figure 26   Edward Shaw, Gothic Churches, plate 51 of *Rural Architecture* (1843). Author's collection.

are the same as his classical models except for a few pointed windows and occasional bargeboards.[131] While he continued to present them, even in perspective views, in isolated linear form without shadows or ambience, and that against his own advice published in *Civil Architecture*, his contemporaries had begun to show their designs in picturesque landscape settings. He had been publishing "builder's guides" aimed at the mechanics while they had introduced the house book or "stylebook" aimed at clients.[132] His weak attempt here to move in that direction showed him to be still mired in the past. Comparison of this book and its slight reworking under the title *The Modern Architect* of 1854 (see #12, below) with Lewis F. Allen's *Rural Architecture* of 1852, a popular work on site-specific

94

Figure 27 Edward Shaw, Gothic Church, ca. 1850, plate 54 of *The Modern Architect*, 1854. Author's collection.

farm houses, farm buildings, and landscape scenically illustrated by Otis & Brown, architects of Buffalo, shows Shaw's engraved plates to be graphically lifeless and dated.

Gilman was not finished: "The Doric cottages . . . may be copied . . . for there is no doubt that they are sufficiently expensive and sufficiently absurd to be at once considered very tasteful; but it is scarcely possible, that any individual can be so misguided as to entertain any predilection for Mr. Shaw's Gothic." College-educated Gilman, who as we know also swung a heavy critical hammer at Shaw's

builder-turned-architect contemporaries such as Isaiah Rogers, was in the fore-
front of the local turn to continental styles, particularly French and Italianate,
and he would smile only on those architects of the next generation who hewed
to that future. The sixth edition of *Civil Architecture* (see #11, below) was to offer
a few designs in the latter style (but they were not designed by Shaw).

Nor had Gilman yet run out of vituperation: "Of Gothic architecture, of the
power and greatness of talent displayed in the ecclesiastical structures of the
Old World . . . Mr. Shaw has, evidently, about as adequate an idea an any quadru-
ped whose name could be selected from the extensive nomenclature of modern
zoology." Yet here is some of what Shaw, perhaps aided by Charles W. Moore,
wrote himself or copied about Gothic in the Introduction to the 1832 and later
editions of *Civil Architecture*: "The column, not being diminished above [as a
classical one would be], and having no entablature, is better suited, in point of
stability, to support the arch springing immediately from it, as only a continuation
of the column. . . . On viewing a Gothic building, we perceive how admirably the
parts are constructed for the eye to embrace the whole." If the quote is not
original to him, the compiler, he was at least astute enough to recognize its virtue.
He understood from a distance the majesty of the European cathedrals, and he
understood that his own churches were not in the same league.

It should be recognized in glossing Gilman's criticism here that he was no
impartial scourge of current architecture, whether it be that of Shaw, Minard
Lafever, or others. As an aspiring architect he was hardly disinterested in the
work of his possible competitors. In a letter to Richard Upjohn, the distinguished
Gothicist whose work he admired, written just one year after his article attacking
Shaw appeared in the *North American Review*, Gilman referred to Lafever's
ecclesiastical work as "'illuminated gothic' which will probably last til [*sic*] he
gets home again—certainly not much longer."[133] Gilman wrote to ask Upjohn to
recommend him to a building committee for an unnamed ecclesiastical commission leaning toward Lafever. "The fear that another valuable job *might* fall into
the hands of the Philistines has induced" him to write.[134] But more cogent to
understanding his slamming of Shaw's domestic work is Gilman's further reference
to his own literary aspiration. He goes on to say that he is engaged on a book
pointedly entitled " 'Rural Residences adopted to North America,' a series of
ten designs for cottages and villas in the English and Italian styles." The plates
were to be finely colored aquatints. It was obviously to be a pointed foil to
Shaw's domestic projects. Apparently the proposed publication never reached
the presses.

Despite Gilman's assessment, Talbot Hamlin later recognized that this title
had "many designs of houses and churches that exerted wide influence. The
popularity of these books [including *Civil Architecture*] perhaps evidences the
growing complexity of the building trades and the greater thoroughness that was
required of builders and architects in this period."[135]

A volume of *Rural Architecture* came to Harvard as a gift from the publisher on October 19, 1843. Another was for sale in Manchester, New Hampshire, by October 1844, and another advertised in the *Louisville Daily Courier* as late as October 1849. The New Hampshire Historical Society copy is signed "Josiah L. Hale / 1844" and "J. L. Hale / 1844." A Josiah Little Hale (1803–75) was a member of a merchant family active in Newbury, Massachusetts–Portsmouth, New Hampshire, area. The Amherst College copy is inscribed by "Stone Picker-ing." The copy in Yale's Beinecke Library is signed "Richard Jones." The American Antiquarian Society copy is inscribed "Owned & used[?] by John Purrington / So. Reading Mass." Purrington is listed under carpenters and builders in the 1852 edition of *The Massachusetts Register*. The copy at the University of Delaware is signed "J. B[?]. Miller." That at the Marquand Library at Princeton reads "Jared Buell Guilford CT" (other inscriptions have been erased). Buell was a joiner by trade in partnership with his nephew, the master-builder William E. Weld. Buell's boxy Italianate house of 1850 still stands on Boston Street, Guilford. The volume in the Kroch Library at Cornell University is stamped "Stationers Hall 1103 King St. Toronto." The copy at the Lilly Library at Indiana University is not signed or dated but has a series of drafted elevations and plans with calculations for a two-story frame house spread over several versos of the plates. It is a design independent of Shaw's models. The copy at the Sherman Library at Dartmouth is inscribed "Samuel E. Petit." "Belfast, Maine" is faintly legible on another page. Petit has thus far avoided further identification. His volume is richly embellished with snatches of religious sentiment copied from William Cowper and small drawings dated in October (18)70. The Bethel Histori-cal Society has a copy inscribed by architect John Kimball of Portland, Maine.

A copy at the University of Virginia is signed by "Dan'l Davis." That at the Canadian Centre for Architecture is inscribed "Jond" or "Jona" " Goldsmith." Perhaps this is Jonathan Goldsmith (1783–1847), master builder and architect working in the Federal and Greek Revival styles in Connecticut, Massachusetts, and the Western Reserve after 1805. It seems he did have copies of Benjamin's and LaFever's works; his houses look nothing like Shaw's designs.[136]

There is no written record that Maine architect Benjamin S. Deane (1790–1867) owned a copy of this work, but he must have had access to one for he based the front elevation of his George Stetson house in Bangor of 1847–48 on Plates 23–24 of this work. Details of the plan, however, he poached from Asher Benjamin's *Practice of Architecture*.[137] The overall form of the Edmiston house of 1845 in West Andover, Ohio, built by Leverett Osborn,[138] reflects the Grecian Ionic house published here, whereas the Doric house might have inspired the general form of the 1840s house in Yellow Springs, Ohio, published by Talbot Hamlin in the *Art Bulletin* for September 1942.[139] It also appears to have been the source for 1846–47 Thomas W. Ward house in Austin, Texas. And the book "seems to offer a prototype" for the recessed portico of the Jacob Conser house of 1854 in Jefferson, Oregon, according to Marion D. Ross, writing in the *Oregon Historical Quarterly* of 1956.

In just this limited survey of one edition of one title, Shaw touched nineteenth-century architects, builders, and others from Canada and Maine to Connecticut and Massachusetts, and from Ohio to Texas to Oregon. And his influence lingered well beyond them, for as late as 1895 Louis H. Gibson praised one of Shaw's domestic designs in his *Beautiful Houses,* and a hundred years later Thomas Gordon Smith had his students at the School of Architecture at Notre Dame building models of Shaw's domestic designs (see Fig. 25).

> 9. *Practical Masonry: / or/ A Theoretical and Operative Treatise of Building; / Containing a / Scientific Account of Stones, Clays, Bricks, Mortars, Cements, Fire-/places, Furnaces, &c.; A Description of Their Component Parts, / with the Manner of Preparing and Using them; / and / the Fundamental Rules in Geometry, / on / Masonry and Stone-Cutting, / with / Their Application to Practice.* Illustrated with Forty-Four Copperplate Engravings. By Edward Shaw, Architect, Author of "Civil Architecture," "Rural Architecture," Etc. Boston: Published by Benjamin B. Mussey. 1846. Registered for copyright, 1845. Quarto. 192 pp., 44 copperplate engravings by W. W. Wilson. William A. Hall, printer, School Street. Hitchcock 1160.

The American Antiquarian Society and New Hampshire Historical Society copies say "Cambridge: Metcalf and Company, Printers to the University." The notice of deposit on the reverse of the title page of the Boston Athenaeum and New Hampshire Historical Society copies have Edward Shaw's name pasted over the original "Thomas H. Webb and Company." *The North American,* November 15, 1845, gives Carey & Hart as the Philadelphia publishers. Thus, three publishers appear to have issued this work, although the contribution of each is not clear: Benjamin B. Mussey (1835–48), an "obscure" Boston publisher who was also issuing Asher Benjamin's books in these years;[140] Carey and Hart, a distinguished Philadelphia house; and Thomas H. Webb and Company of Boston, the publisher of the popular Rollo series of boy's books. This is effectively a second edition of *Operative Masonry* (see #4, above) physically enlarged to the size of the architectural books (Fig. 28). There are four additional plates. As a "practical" work, however, this was not presented as richly as some of those on architecture but in full or half calf with a label reading SHAW'S / MASONRY on the spine.

The adjectives *practical* and *operative* are reversed on the title pages of Shaw's two books on masonry. Because they are two ways of saying much the same thing according to definitions in the 1845 edition of Webster's *American Dictionary,* in general applying to some useful action, why did Shaw change the adjective

PRACTICAL MASONRY:

OR

A THEORETICAL AND OPERATIVE TREATISE OF BUILDING:

CONTAINING A

SCIENTIFIC ACCOUNT OF STONES, CLAYS, BRICKS, MORTARS, CEMENTS, FIRE
PLACES, FURNACES, &c.; A DESCRIPTION OF THEIR COMPONENT PARTS,
WITH THE MANNER OF PREPARING AND USING THEM,

AND

THE FUNDAMENTAL RULES IN GEOMETRY,

ON

MASONRY AND STONE-CUTTING,

WITH

THEIR APPLICATION TO PRACTICE.

ILLUSTRATED WITH FORTY-FOUR COPPERPLATE ENGRAVINGS.

BY EDWARD SHAW, ARCHITECT,

AUTHOR OF "CIVIL ARCHITECTURE," "RURAL ARCHITECTURE," ETC.

BOSTON:
PUBLISHED BY BENJAMIN B. MUSSEY.
1846.

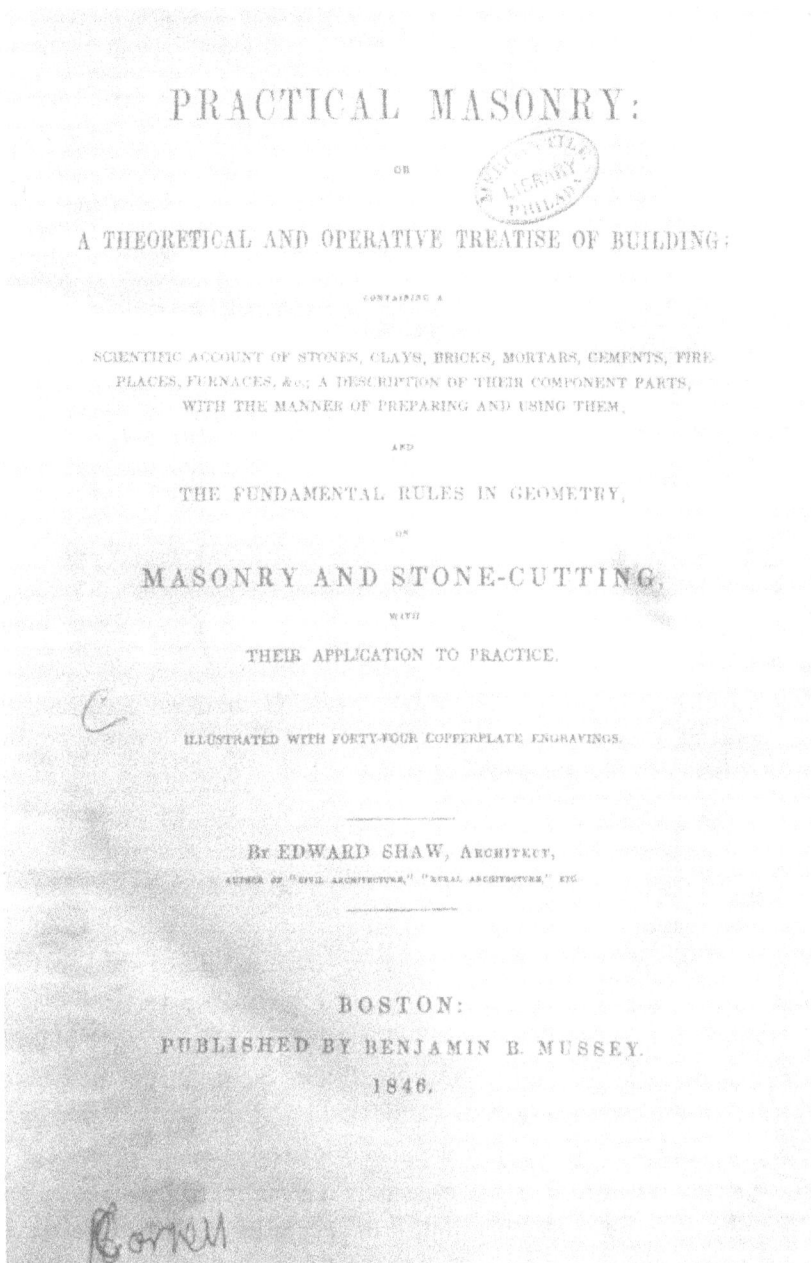

Figure 28   Edward Shaw, title page to *Practical Masonry*, 1846. Author's collection.

in the title here? Or change the size from royal octavo to quarto? Or fail to mention the earlier work among his previous publications listed after his name on the title page? Did he (or his publishers) hope this would be seen as a new book? Reviewers treated it as such.

It would seem that Shaw did not make the change because of the Freemasons' use of the *Operative Masonry* phrase, which so often appears in the Masonic press during these years, as did the term *Practical Masonry*, the title of an article in the *American Masonic Register* for June 6, 1840. But as the author was an acquaintance of Charles W. Moore, his use of these titles may have been more than an accidental coincidence. *The Practice of Masonry* would have been a more descriptive choice, and it does occur in one misnomer in the press in reference to this title. Of course, Shaw may have simply chosen this title in emulation of Peter Nicolson's *Practical Masonry, Bricklaying, and Plastering* of 1830. Shaw here quotes verbatim Nicholson's remarks on "Atkinson's Cement."

The Preface is unchanged from *Operative Masonry*. Chapters IV and V are rewritten. Added subjects include scagiola and its composition (briefly mentioned as early as his *Civil Architecture* in 1832 (see #3), three Grecian orders only, a table of weights and measures, and a glossary of architectural terms. In Chapter V, Shaw added an illustrated section on "Warming by Steam and Hot Water" and another "On the Construction of Ovens, Boilers, Fireplaces, and of the Setting of Copper" that enlarge on the treatment in *Operative Masonry*. These include Benjamin Blaney's water furnace for warming dwelling houses. For Plate 32, a method of fixing up a copper boiler for brewing, Shaw followed the lead of David Booth, probably from his *The Art of Brewing* of 1829 (Booth was a polymath member of London's Society for the Diffusion of Useful Knowledge and, as Shaw says, the author of many books.) He mentions (Jacob?) Perkins's patent cooking range although he prefers hot water and illustrates the apparatus installed by a Mr. Dexter in S(amuel) K(ing) Williams's house, 68 Boylston Street, Boston. It had features similar to the Bryant and Hermann furnace Shaw had specified for his Warren house of 1840, his Sears house of 1842, and illustrated here. Other devices mentioned and illustrated are (H. & F.) Stimson's patent radiating and hot air cooking range, and the improved coal oven for bakers installed in various parts of Europe under the direction of "Mr. Elms, the architect," perhaps one of the Elmes family of England.

Shaw's treatment of his subject continued to receive positive reviews. The *Boston Recorder* for April 9, 1846, especially recommended the book to young masons "who aspire to distinction in their calling in life. . . . [It] contains, so to speak, the literature and science of their branch of industry . . . [so] let them make the study of this work the occupation of their leisure hours." Hitchcock lists no American competitors to either of Shaw's works on masonry construction.

The book was advertised in the *Pittsburgh Daily Post* for November 25, 1845. It was for sale in New Orleans by April 1849 (*The Daily Crescent*), and in Tennessee, by March1853 (*Nashville Union*). The copy at the University of Delaware is signed (twice) "J. A. Hamblin Farmington Falls Maine," and stamped J. A. HAMBLIN / MASON. It is also signed by "Lizzie Hamblin / Sept 11. 1876."

John Abbott Hamblin (b. 1818) is listed as a mason in the 1850 U. S. Census, and a master mason in the 1860 U. S. Census. The Boston Athenaeum copy was given by Edward E. Pratt, November 15, 1881. One Edward E. Pratt was treasurer of the Associated Charities of Boston that year. It is also inscribed on the second free leaf: "J. H. Brooks" or "J. W. Brooks" or "John Brooks." The New Hampshire Historical Society copy is signed "Sam'l Hame [?] / Dover" (?). The copy in the Fine Arts Library at the University of Pennsylvania contains the name of "Samuel S[t]an[le]y [?], Salem Mass." That in the Kroch Library at Cornell University is stamped several times MERCANTILE LIBRARY PHILADA in an oval. According to that library's catalogue, this title entered its collection between 1857 and 1860. The bookplate in the copy at the Library Company of Philadelphia indicates that is was purchased in 1856.

10. *Rural Architecture: / Consisting of / Classic Dwellings, / Doric, Ionic, Corinthian and Gothic, / and / Details Connected with each of the Orders; / Embracing / Plans, Elevations Parallel and Perspective, / Specifications, Estimates, Framing, Etc. / for / Private Houses and Churches, / to which is added a / Modern System of Stair Building.* Illustrated by Sixty Copper Plat Engravings. By Edward Shaw, Architect, Author of Civil Architecture, Operative Masonry, etc. Second Edition, Revised and Enlarged. Boston, James B. Dow, 1850. Registered for copyright, 1843, by Edward Shaw. William A. Hall, printer, 23 School Street. William W. Wilson plates. Quarto. 121 pp., 60 pls. Not in Hitchcock.

This second edition, heretofore recognized in only one copy at the Avery Library, Columbia University, has now been joined by a second in the library of the Maine Historical Society, Portland. The Maine copy collates exactly with the Avery copy. Both have two identical plates numbered 47, one opposite the title page acting as a frontispiece, the other in its proper place. In both known copies, plate 58 is bound in upside down!

Through the kindness of Teresa Harris of the Avery Library, who compared the New York copy with one of the first edition, it can be said that this (aborted?) second edition contains numerous changes from the first (see #8, above). The title omits the reference to the United States of America. The mention of stair building in the title is new and is noted (out of numerical sequence) in the Table of Contents: "Stair Building (Plates) p. 100." This section occupies pages 100 to 116, and in part refers to unexplained plates present in some copies of the first edition. The text of the first edition ends at page 98. Here additional pages and plates have been added to Church Architecture. Pages 99–100 refer to Plates 53–56 (a gothic church: Plate 53: Front Elevation; Plate 54: Side Elevation; Plate 55: Ground Plan, Gallery, Ceiling, Transverse Section; Plate 56: Portion of Front Finish of Galleries; Longitudinal Section; Elevation of the Front Pews, Panels and Scrole [sic]; Longitudinal Section; Vertical Section of Tower Column. This would reappear in *The Modern Architect* (see #12, below). The Glossary at the end of the first edition, already set up at the printer's, is placed in the second edition after the section on Stair Building although the pagination is unchanged from the earlier edition: it begins at 99 and continues to 108.

With such careless bookmaking it is no wonder that the 1850 version is rare. These copies were not just mock-ups for an edition that never materialized, however. The issue got some distribution because both the *Chronicle* and the *Journal* of Wilmington, North Carolina, ran ads for this title, most likely in this edition, in March 1850. Another appeared in *The Daily Dispatch* of Richmond, Virginia, in October 1854. And the Avery copy is signed "J. Preston," whereas the Maine copy is signed "Winslow Alden's Book Boston Mass." A note on the frontispiece (Plate 47) of the latter copy, in the same hand as the signature, identifies the depicted David Sears II house as being in Brookline and costing $8000 (the figure cited in Shaw's text), and the same comment is repeated under the views of the house on plates 47 and 48, so Alden seems to have been particularly interested in that local example of Shaw's executed architecture. The Maine copy comes from the architectural library of Portland architect John Calvin Stevens. He was in Boston in 1880 supervising the construction of the Hotel Pemberton at Nantasket Beach for the architect Francis Fassett. During his eighteen months in the area he also assisted the architect Winslow Alden. Family tradition has it that Alden paid Stevens in books from his own library, presumably including the copy of *Rural Architecture* now in the Portland collection.[141]

11. *Shaw's / Civil Architecture; /Being / A Complete Theoretical and Practical / System of Building, / Containing / The Fundamental Principles of the Art, / Illustrated by Eighty-Two Copperplate Engravings. / By Edward Shaw, Architect / Sixth Edition, Revised and Improved. / To which are added / Twenty Copperplate Engravings, / also, / A Treatise on Gothic Architecture, with Plates, &c / By Thomas W. Silloway and George M. Harding, / Architects.* Boston: Published by John P. Jewett and Company; Cleveland: Jewett, Proctor, and Worthington, MDCCCLII. Registered for copyright, 1852, by Luther Stevens. Stereotyped at the Boston Stereotype Company (in some copies). Quarto. 191 pp., 102 pls. Hitchcock 1149.

For Luther Stevens see the entry for *Civil Architecture*, 1832 (#3, above). It is not clear why he is again listed as the register for copyright because he appears to have had nothing else to do with this edition. Nineteen new plates were noted by Hitchcock, with G. G. Smith as engraver. George Girdler Smith (1795–1878) is probably best remembered for his engraved copy of the famed 1722 "Bonner" map of Boston. With this edition of this title, the page and plate count reached

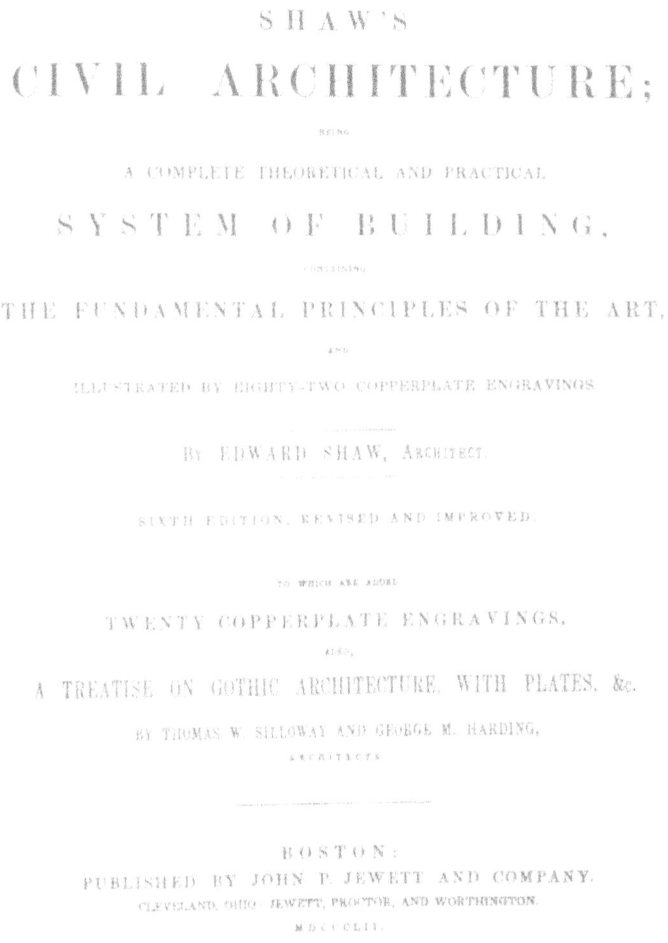

SHAW'S

CIVIL ARCHITECTURE;

BEING

A COMPLETE THEORETICAL AND PRACTICAL

SYSTEM OF BUILDING,

CONTAINING

THE FUNDAMENTAL PRINCIPLES OF THE ART,

AND

ILLUSTRATED BY EIGHTY-TWO COPPERPLATE ENGRAVINGS

BY EDWARD SHAW, ARCHITECT

SIXTH EDITION, REVISED AND IMPROVED.

TO WHICH ARE ADDED

TWENTY COPPERPLATE ENGRAVINGS,

ALSO,

A TREATISE ON GOTHIC ARCHITECTURE, WITH PLATES, &c.

BY THOMAS W. SILLOWAY AND GEORGE M. HARDING,

ARCHITECTS

BOSTON:
PUBLISHED BY JOHN P. JEWETT AND COMPANY.
CLEVELAND, OHIO: JEWETT, PROCTOR, AND WORTHINGTON.
MDCCCLII.

Figure 29   Edward Shaw, title page to *Shaw's Civil Architecture,* sixth edition, Boston: John P. Jewett and Company, 1852. Author's collection.

its final form. A new publisher appears in Boston. John Punchard Jewett started the company in 1847, and also acquired the rights to publish the book version of *Uncle Tom's Cabin* at this time.[142] The Cleveland branch was established in 1851 (Fig. 29).

The decorative binding for *Rural Architecture* (see #8, above) is repeated here. The front cover has the gold-stamped image of the Nativity. The spine bears, also gold-stamped, top to bottom, a square composition of carpenters' tools with one pair of draftsman's dividers, SHAW'S / CIVIL / ARCHITECTURE, a perspectival rendering of a Gothic church tower and spire unlike those in Shaw's plates in *Rural Architecture* and *The Modern Architect*, and JOHN P. JEWETT & CO. Did Shaw design these images? The Gothic ecclesiastical architecture is rather more Upjohnian than Shavian. The image of the mechanic's tools harks back to the author's beginnings; he had switched his intended readership to architects and clients with his *Rural Architecture*. As Hammatt Billings illustrated Jewett's contemporary book for Stowe, which appeared with a front cover gold-stamped with a view of Tom's cabin after one of Billings's illustrations, we might suppose that artist-architect designed the cover art here. But, because it is only tangentially related to the content of the book, as noted above, it is more than likely that the Nativity was picked from some engraver's or binder's existing stock. Such a handsomely presented book was surely not intended to be carried onto the job site but to be used for study at home or in a library, or, perhaps, to be placed at eye-level in the bookcase of a bibliophile.

The advertisement in this edition repeats that of the first, but Shaw added a note dated January 1, 1852: "I have been induced by the advice of my friends to secure the valuable services of Messrs. Silloway and Harding, architects of Boston, gentlemen well versed in the science they profess, to assist in revising the fifth edition [now unknown (see #7, above), if it ever existed it would have been issued in the 1840s when both Silloway and Harding were in their late teens], and prepare additional drawings for the sixth, which has resulted in the exclusion of several of the old plates, and the substitution of twenty new ones of a character in keeping with the improvements of the day, and of great practical use to the carpenter and builder, among which are four plates of Gothic details selected from Pugin [*Specimens of Gothic Architecture*, which Shaw mentions elsewhere], one of the best English authors on the subject." This is the last of Shaw's books for which he appears to have written all the introductory matter. Because that is dated on the first day of the year of publication, he probably wrote this material late in 1851.

The title-page reference to Vitruvius et al. has now disappeared, and there are other important changes to the previous text. Silloway and Harding did contribute the essay on Gothic, signing as "The Editors," and, if they were also, as is likely, "The Editors" who "revived and improved" the book by rearranging the composition of the earlier editions and adding or substituting new material to Shaw's previous editions in the form of several new footnotes, text, and plates, then they had a very significant role in the production of this, the definitive edition. It was this version that, when he reprinted it several times to the end of the century, Henry Carey Baird listed as the work of "Messrs. Shaw, Silloway & Harding" (see #18, below).

Thomas William Silloway (1828–1910), a student of Ammi B. Young from 1847, began his own practice in 1851, so it might be supposed that Young recommended his student for the job of significantly revising and improving Shaw's title. What Shaw thought of this we do not know despite his note in the advertisement. Silloway was to develop into a prolific New England architect, primarily of churches (he would also become a Unitarian minister). In 1858 he published in Boston an illustrated *Text-Book of Modern Carpentry*, in which, among Bostonians, he mentions Asher Benjamin, Alexander Parris, C. G. Hall, and Richard Bond, but not Shaw, who had left the city by then, although (or perhaps because) the two cover some of the same subjects, including bridges, in their books (see Chapter 1). Little seems to be known about the previous preparation of George Milford Harding (1827–1910). His association with Silloway dissolved in 1853 when he formed a partnership with J. L. Foster. Shaw joined Young and others as "referees" endorsing that firm (*New Hampshire Patriot* for November 9 of that year). Harding eventually practiced in Maine. Silloway and Harding's work on this edition, including some new text and new plates, thus stemmed from 1851–52. In those years Jewett nudged aside sixty-seven-year-old Shaw and brought in two fledging, twenty-something architects to rework his book. This is made obvious in an article in the *Eastern Argus* for May 29, 1852, in which the pair is lauded for drawings added to Shaw's book.

The reaching out to a younger generation apparently better steeped in Gothic design may have been a rather belated reaction to Arthur Gilman's scathing criticism of Shaw's knowledge of the Gothic in his 1844 review of *Rural Architecture* (see #8, above). Shaw attributes the move to the urging of unnamed friends, but his new publisher may have also encouraged it and other changes in order to brighten up a dimming product. The earlier plates showing country Gothic churches are now gone. Shaw did not design what replaced them. Silloway and Harding's scholarly essay on "Gothic, or what may be termed, with more propriety, English architecture," clearly indicates their reading on the development of the medieval style. They cite a number of references, including, judging by the truncated names given, John Henry Parker's *Glossary of Architecture*, 1850 edition; the Rev. James Dallaway's *A Series of Discourses upon Architecture*, 1834; Thomas Rickman's *An Attempt to Discriminate the Styles of English Architecture*, 1817; A. C. Pugin's *Specimens*; Joseph Gwilt, surely his *Encyclopaedia of Architecture*, first edition 1842; John Britton's *Cathedral Antiquities of England* (1814–35); the Rev. George Millers's *Description of the Cathedral Church of Ely*, 1807; and a "Mr. Henry" on cathedrals, whose identity has so far escaped detection. There is a table of comparative dimensions of English cathedrals, and four plates of Gothic details copied from Pugin. Oddly, there is nothing in their essay concerning the modern use of the Gothic style. It is, rather, preceded by plates credited to Silloway and Harding showing A. C. Mayhew's rural villa and the Pearl Street Universalist Society Meeting House, both in Milford, Massachusetts, both dated 1850, both designed by Silloway and Harding, with a long description of the meetinghouse by Silloway. And both are in Gilman's preferred Italianate style, and perhaps intended to smooth or ward off another scathing review.

With this edition Shaw begins to lose control of his opus. The new plates noted by Hitchcock, some alterations to the old ones, are credited to "Silloway & Harding" as delineators. They show the classical orders and some windowframes and doorframes and an oriel window, so the pair was not charged only with bringing Shaw's Gothic up to date. They revised or added to a sizeable portion of this edition. Clearly our author had worn out his relevance and lost control of his material. His same loss of grip also seems to have occurred with the publication, fast on the heels of this one, of his *The Modern Architect* (see #12, below).

The section on bridges now includes a description of a model of a "Tubular Suspension Bridge" patented by Ammi White of Boston, which was endorsed by "The Editors." White, "a plain unlettered mechanic of New Hampshire" invented in the late 1840s and patented in 1852 a wooden substitute for wire cable that would give the strength of iron but avoid the rust. (Beginning in the late 1830s, Charles Ellet had been proposing wire suspension bridges and in 1842 erected the first such span across the Schuylkill river in Philadelphia.) White showed his model around the country for a number of years and received much notice in the press. It was reported to be capable of providing a bridge to span the Ohio River at Cincinnati. (The Kentucky General Assembly granted a charter for such a bridge in 1846. It was ultimately realized in iron by John Roebling after the Civil War.) A bridge of White's design did connect the two much closer halves of Boston's triennial Charitable Mechanic Association's eighth exhibition of 1856 divided between Faneuil Hall and Quincy Market.[143] White vanishes from available news coverage thereafter. Shaw's interest in bridge design dates to the earliest editions of this title, and here he—if it was him—inserted a notice that refers to one of the latest innovations.

The *Boston Evening Transcript* for May 18, 1853, says of this edition that it "combines so many excellent properties, that economy, if no higher object be contemplated, should induce both owners and builders of estates to consult it. . . . [T]he more extensively it is circulated, the greater will be the advantages accruing to the towns and cities in New England, in respect to the fine architectural display, as wealth and population increases."

For sale in St. Louis by May 1854 (*Tri-Weekly Missouri Republican*), in Wheeling, West Virginia, as a "new book" in April 1854 (*Wheeling Daily Intelligencer*), in Richmond, Virginia, as a "new edition" in October 1854 (*The Daily Dispatch*), and in Chicago by January 21, 1857 (*Chicago Daily Tribune*). The copy at Notre Dame is signed "James Leavitt, Portland, Me." He is listed as a joiner in the city directory for 1850. The copy at the Avery Library, once the property of Henry-Russell Hitchcock, contains the business card of George M. Harding,

Scollay's Building, Boston, giving as references A. B. Young, Dr. B. B. Appleton, and George G. Smith, Esq. That copy is inscribed "George Holbrook [?] / Brookline [Mass.] 1853" as well as "James G. Robinson." As with many copies of Shaw's books, this one was at some point used to press fern leaves. The copy at the Canadian Centre for Architecture has a label reading "General Society of Mechanics & Tradesmen, Apprentices' Library, New York," accompanied by an arm and hammer logo. It is also stamped DE MILT LIBRARY / G.S.M.& T.N.Y. in a red oval. The Apprentices' was a lending library, the De Milt for reference only. This volume is listed in the *Catalogue of the Apprentices' and De Milt Libraries* dated July 1, 1855. The copy in the library at Winterthur is inscribed on the front endpaper, "Presented to / Samuel N. Newcomb / of Lynnfield / by / Nath'l S. Dearborn / of South Reading / January 1st 1853." It is also inscribed "Worthington / 1852." Newcomb was a carpenter; Nathaniel Sigourney Dearborn (1814–91) was an engraver and printer in Boston as was his father (1786–1852), also Nathaniel. The son was a member of the Massachusetts Charitable Mechanic Association.

The American Antiquarian Society copy has the gold-stamped Nativity scene on the cover. Inside is the inscription "Otis A. Merrill / Haverhill Mass/ Feb 13th 1867" and a bookplate: "ARCHITECTURAL LIBRARY / OF / OTIS A. MERRILL /Lowell, Mass." There are a few slight pencil sketches. Merrill (b. 1844) worked as a carpenter in Haverhill for a few years after mustering out of the Union Army as a decorated hero; he then moved to Lowell to practice architecture. After 1883 he joined Arthur S. Cutler (b. 1854) in partnership. Merrill & Cutler was an active local firm through the end of the century. Their City Hall in Lowell (1890–94), a commission won in competition, is an impressive example of the Romanesque Revival.[144] Among their many other buildings, the Colonial Revival/Shingle Style Henry Bradford Lewis House in Andover, Massachusetts, of 1897–98 is listed on the National Register of Historic Places.

The copy at Pennsylvania State University is unsigned but has a long, handwritten text scrawled over several pages. It is poetry that seems to have been copied from the *Memoir of Edward Mott Woolley* (1855). That at Rutgers University is inscribed "Wm G. Morse," most likely William Gilbert Morse (b. 1829) of Bangor, Maine, a skilled draftsman and precocious designer who did not join the Mechanic Association but in a burst of youthful creative energy provided his native city with designs for the chapel of the Theological Seminary (1851–58), the Columbia Street Baptist Church (1853), and Norumbega Market Hall (1854–55) as well as numerous houses. His drawings (1855) for the Congregational Church on Isle au Haut survive.[145] He did not follow Shaw's lead in ecclesiastical design. His later years are lost to history.

A copy of this edition in the author's possession is inscribed variously "Grady D. Harmon," (a South Carolina surname), "W. A. Swanson / Mayberry Springs

[Inn?] / Hot Springs Arkansas," "E. J.[?] White—[CE?] Archt / March 1857," and a stamped address (twice) with the name obliterated: "206-B Cassin St. Liberty Homes / North Charleston S. Carolina." None of these inscriptions has yielded to identification. A copy for sale by J. B. Muns Fine Arts Books in 2015 has stamps of R. S. Beetley and William F. Stone Jr. as well as "Aug 6/54 $6.00" written in ink, all on the title page. The first was most likely Robert S. Beetley of Baltimore (ca. 1820–96) whose biography is traceable through various sources, including the *Baltimore Sun*. It reads as one of continually upward achievement in a variety of occupations related to building. Born in Alexandria, Virginia, he was first a ship joiner and teacher of navigation. He appears as a bookkeeper in 1860, as a City Commissioner in 1861, a house carpenter in 1865, an architect in 1867, a commissioner of the city's Jones' Falls Improvement Project in 1872, and Inspector of Public Buildings in 1878. William F. Stone, Jr. was an Art Deco Baltimore architect. In the 1950s, he served as architect for the Episcopal diocese of Maryland.

According to its catalogue, a copy of this edition entered the collection of the Mercantile Library Company of Philadelphia by 1856. In that year "S. R. Kirby," East Saginaw, Michigan, richly scrolled his signature in his copy of this edition. It is now in the Dartmouth College library. New York-born Stephen R. Kirby (1824–1906) became a well-known builder and engineer after years of sailing on Lake Michigan, rising from cabin boy to ship's captain. By 1853 in East Saginaw, he had begun building boats, continued sailing, and took charge of construction of the Bancroft House, a hotel completed in 1859. For that endeavor he must have acquired Shaw's book for guidance, although the building itself seems to have owed much to Isaiah Rogers's recent Midwestern hotels. Kirby went on to design and build lake boats and grain elevators.[146]

12. *The / Modern Architect; / or, / Every Carpenter his own Master. / Embracing / Plans, Elevations, Specifications, Framing, Etc., / for / Private Houses, Classic Dwellings, Churches, &c. / to which is added / The New System of Stair-Building.* By Edward Shaw. Illustrated by Sixty-five Engravings by W. W. Wilson and George G. Smith. Boston: Dayton and Wentworth, 86 Washington St., 1854. Registered for copyright, 1854, by Dayton & Wentworth. Stereotyped by Hobart & Robbins, New England Type and Stereotype Foundry, Boston / Damrell and Moore, Printers, 16 Devonshire St., Boston (American Antiquarian Society copy). Geo. C. Rand, Printer (Hay Library copy). Quarto. 128 pp., 64 pls. (plus Frontispiece.) Bound in after plates: "The New Lien Law of Massachusetts in Favor of Mechanics, Passed in 1851, with all the Amendments in full to 1853." Hitchcock 1156.

Not to be confused with *The Modern Architect*, a series of "original designs" by Oliver P. Smith that appeared in Buffalo this same year. That series lasted but one issue.[147]

"present" in the introductory material of his titles. There is a footnote to the Preface signed by him dated May 15, 1854, the year this edition was deposited. As noted in Chapter 1, it contains a wooly interpretation of Shaw's career. It seems to have first appeared printed on paper different from the rest of the book and tipped into the copy now in the Library Company in Philadelphia, for example, and certainly others. (It was later incorporated into the letterpress with a different typeface.) A descriptive notice of this new title appeared in the *Boston Evening Transcript* for May 18, 1853, a year earlier than the registry of copyright and Shaw's dated statement, suggesting that the footnote could have been added to answer questions about his qualifications that arose from advanced copies. As noted above, Shaw seems to have been losing his grip on his books by the time of the sixth edition of *Civil Architecture* (see #11, above), which appeared some two years earlier. He apparently left Boston about this time. Although the given information is too speculative to generate a clear statement, it may be that he had less to do with the appearance of this revision of *Rural Architecture* than has been recognized.

The Publisher's Preface is addressed to "every Mechanic deserving the name of Carpenter, who may have a desire to become his own master . . . . In the opinion of good judges, the present work has not been excelled for minuteness of detail, and practical application to the wants of the practical man." The work is addressed to the Mechanic, the Master, and the Architect, and includes the "Ancient and Modern foundation principles and systems of the Egyptian, Grecian, Corinthian, Doric, Ionic and Gothic modes of building." A "pure Architectural taste is a great gift," it continues, "and, if this science were more generally studied . . . we should be exempt from those architectural abortions which now so often disgrace our cities and villages."

The May 1853, notice of this title is headed "Shaw's Architecture." It says that a "treatise on this important subject has been written" and "the more extensively it is circulated, the greater will be the advantages accruing to the towns and cities in New England, in respect to the progress of a refined architectural display, as wealth and population increases." In the *Cabinet* of Schenectady, New York, on July 25, 1854, Dayton and Wentworth ran an ad on the same day the paper published notice of the new work: "A fortune can be made by selling 'The Modern Architect' . . . Agents wanted to circulate this valuable publication in every City, Town and Village in the United States." It will become "a Standard Work, on this science, for the next one hundred years."

The Weekly Wisconsin of Milwaukee noticed this first edition in early February 1854. The *Western Reserve Chronicle* of Warren, Ohio, ran an ad in February 1855. The copy at the Sawyer Library, Williams College, has a very faded inscription on the first free leaf that might include the name H. C. Darcey. That at the University of Virginia is signed (twice) by M. C. Abbott and dated 1854.

That at the Hay Library, Brown University (*ex-libris* William H. Jordy) is signed "Isaiah M. Buzzell / Manchester / NH" and "J. M. Buzzell" with a large, curvilinear, calligraphic drawing of a bird. It is also signed twice "S. J. Berard." The copy at the New Hampshire Historical Society is inscribed "Purchased P. K. Foley Dec 1, 1932."

The owner of the copy of this edition at the Lilly Library, Duke University, was not content with signing the book within (although he did that too, twice). On the front cover, beneath the gold-stamped version of Wilson's frontispiece, we find his name gold-stamped in block letters: THOMAS C. VAN REYPER (see Fig. 31). He also inscribed it in large, flourishing script on the front flyleaf; the name of his wife, Mrs. Caroline S[peer] Van Reyper, daughter of the family that founded Upper Montclair, New Jersey, appears in more modest script. Pasted to an early page is an engraving of Trinity Church, New York, finished in 1846. On a rear flyleaf is a semiskillful drawing of a horse. Thomas Cadmus Van Reyper (1833–1909) was a New Jersey farmer and master builder. His 1872 Italianate house, on the campus of Montclair State University and now called the Van Reyper–Bond house, is listed on the National Register of Historic Places.

Plates 13–14 here (or, less likely, in *Rural Architecture*) were the inspiration for the Lorenzo Ling house of 1856 in Pulaski, Oswego County, New York.[148] The original main entrance to the Iowa County Courthouse in Dodgeville, Wisconsin, 1858–59, was copied line for line from Plate 4 according to the application to the National Register of Historic Places (Figs. 32–33). Pls. 53 through 56 show Shaw's version of a modern Gothic church, the exterior treatment of which related to his elevation for the Boston Athenaeum and related designs (see Chapter 2).

13. ***Civil Architecture***. Seventh, Eighth, and Ninth editions; unknown. Hitchcock 1153; see #15, below.)

14. ***The Modern Architect***, etc.: Reprint, Dayton and Wentworth, 1855. Registered for copyright, 1854, by Dayton and Wentworth. Printed by Hobart & Robbins New England Type and Stereograph Foundry, Boston. Quarto. 128 pp; 65 pls. including frontispiece. Hitchcock 1157.

The frontispiece is repeated from the first edition, including the Dayton & Wentworth credit, but dated 1855. Many copies have a gold-stamped image of the frontispiece on the cover; filigreed spine, marbled end papers and fore edges. The "New Lien Law" is included.

It was probably this issue that was advertised in the *Western Reserve Chronicle*, Warren, Ohio, in March 1855. The Getty Research Institute copy is inscribed "G. Taggert [or Taggart, hi]s Book 1856." The Avery Library copy is inscribed by William Ober, Jr., Corry, Pa. Ober, son of a bricklayer, is listed as a carpenter on the 1870 census. The copy in the Ricker Library, University of Illinois, is

Figure 32 Edward Shaw, Grecian frontispiece, Plate 4 of *The Modern Architect*, 1854. Author's Collection.

signed John P. Mcleone [?} / C. Nation [?]." The American Antiquarian Society copy came from the Charles A. Place Estate in December 1941. The copy in the library at Winterthur is inscribed on the front flyleaf "Presented to S. W. Schermerhorn / By his Father / Watertown N.Y. / August 12th 1883." From the

Figure 33 Frontispiece, Iowa County Courthouse, Dodgeville, Wisconsin, 1859. Historic American Building Survey, Library of Congress.

family genealogy compiled by Richard Schermerhorn (1914), it can be deduced that the father was Jason Beebe Schermerhorn (1819–98), a resident of Watertown in the 1870s and 1880s, who in 1884 largely financed the erection of the Emmanuel Congregational Church there; the son was Schuyler W. (1846–after 1914). He is listed as a carpenter on the 1910 Census.

A battered copy recently given to the Lake County Historical Museum in Crown Point, Indiana, is signed "Edgar C. Wheeler" on the second free leaf, and

"John Wheeler / Crown Point / Lake County / Indiana / Aug 1856" on the third (and repeated on the third last free leaf). A note on Plate 48 labels the perspective of the Sears house the "Finest Specimen." There is an amateurish drawing of a mother and child on the verso of the frontispiece, and childish outlines of trains and strange farm (?) animals throughout the book. John Wheeler (1825–63) was a farmer, teacher, county surveyor, and journalist who founded the *Crown Point Register.* He was killed in action on July 2, 1863, at Gettysburg as a colonel of the 20th Regiment of Indiana Volunteers. His memory survives locally in the name of a Crown Point middle school.

15. ***Civil Architecture,*** etc*:* Tenth Edition, Boston: John P. Jewett and Company; Cleveland: Jewett, Procter, and Worthington, MDCCCLVI, registered for copyright, 1852. Quarto. 191 pp., 102 pls. Hitchcock 1153.

As copies of the putative seventh, eighth, and ninth editions have never been found, one wonders if Jewett labelled this number ten to suggest that the title had been more popular that it was.

The copy in the Fine Arts Library at the University of Pennsylvania is ornately inscribed by Vincent S. Minnerly (1845–1913) of Mt. Vernon, New York, and Elmer E. Minnerly (b. 1871) of Mt. Vernon and Brooklyn, his son. Both are listed as real estate brokers in the 1910 U. S. Census. According to the bookplate in the copy at the Library Company of Philadelphia, it was the "Gift of Dr. James Rush / To the Ridgeway Branch / of the / Philadelphia Library / A.D. 1869." Rush, a wealthy shareholder who died that year, left the library his estate with which the Company built its new building on South Broad Street.

16. ***The Modern Architect,*** etc.: Reprint, Boston: Wentworth and Company, 1856. Registered for copyright, 1854, by Dayton & Wentworth. Stereotyped by Hobart & Robbins New England Type and Stereograph Foundry, Boston. 128 pp., 64 plates plus frontispiece. Hitchcock 1158 (with incorrect publisher's name).

Same publisher; new name. The frontispiece retains the 1855 date and Dayton & Wentworth credit.

The University of California copy has "J. Fitzer" stamped on its title the page. In 2015, the copy on the market from James Cummins Bookseller was formerly owned by C. A. Newell. One C. A. Newell is listed as a builder in Little Falls, New York, in *The Architect, Builder and Wood-Worker* for February 1880. The copy at the University of Virginia is signed "Henry L. Lyman / Buffalo / N.Y. / Sept. 15th. 1864." Lyman is listed in Buffalo city directories as a railroad man in the 1860s and 1870s.

17. *The Modern Architect*, etc.: Boston: Wentworth, Hewes & Co., 1859. Registered for copyright, 1854, by Dayton & Wentworth. 128 pp., 65 pls. including frontispiece. Not in Hitchcock.

Same publisher; new name. The (printing of?) the undated frontispiece is now credited to Thayer & Eldridge. The Boston firm of William Wilde Thayer (1829–96) and Charles W. Eldridge (1837–1903) at 114–116 Washington Street existed from late 1859 to early 1861. They issued the third edition of *Leaves of Grass*.[149]

The copy of this scarce reprint in the library of the General Society of Mechanics & Tradesmen in New York City has the red oval stamp of the organization on its title page as does the book at the Canadian Centre for Architecture in Montreal. The latter is also signed with a flourish: "Albert Foster's / Book / 1860."

18. *Civil Architecture*, etc.: Eleventh Edition, Philadelphia: Henry Carey Baird, 1870. Registered for copyright, 1852, by Luther Stevens; registered for copyright, 1869, by Henry Carey Baird. Quarto. 191 pp., 102 pls. "finely engraved on copper." Hitchcock 1154.

This title is listed under Announcements in the *American Literary Gazette and Publishers' Circular* for October 15, 1869. The Preface, dated November 1, 1869, and signed with the publisher's initials, states that "Messrs. Shaw, Silloway & Harding's CIVIL ARCHITECTURE, having been for several years out of print, the present publisher has undertaken the publication of a new edition, and he cannot but feel great confidence that a work of such high character and real practical value, will prove eminently acceptable and useful to American Architects and Builders. As in the past, so in the future, he believes that it must hold a position as one of the most popular books on the subject published in this country."

A Philadelphia publisher takes over here. John P. Jewett, publisher of the immediately previous editions, sold his company in 1857 to Crosby and Nichols. Henry Carey Baird, grandson of noted publisher Mathew Carey, reorganized his ancestor's firm under his own name in 1849. He then published scientific and practical books "in an effort to further native American manufactures" according to Charles B. Wood III. Shaw had been dead for a decade, but Silloway and/or Harding, listed equally here with Shaw as creators, may have been in a position to license this edition.

From a review of new publications in Chicago's *American Builder and Journal of Art*, January 1, 1870: "The book, which has been out of print for a number of years, again makes its appearance, looking fresher and more beautiful than ever. . . . [J]udging from its past popularity, and the faithful manner in which the present publisher has performed his work, we are confident it must meet with a large sale. While it is a work that will always find a welcome place in every architect's library, it is nevertheless sufficiently elementary in character to be sought after by every architectural student. . . . There seems to be at the present time a large demand for architectural publications, whose only value consists in plans and detailed drawings, while they may not contain a single original idea. . . . This work . . . is worth . . . many times its price [$10.00]. . . . A volume of this kind furnishes a man with ideas. It gives him tools to work with. . . . We have no hesitancy in saying" to any not possessing this work, "that they will consult their best interests by purchasing it."

According to the *Scientific American* (January 8, 1870): "A work of this character which can reach eleven editions scarcely needs other evidence of its worth. As its title imports, it is not a mere collection of designs of little value to any but the finished designer, but a complete elementary treatise, beginning at the foundation of the science; and after taking the reader by pleasant and easy gradations through the first principles, teaching him how to apply them to actual work. . . . The whole work has been thoroughly and carefully revised [!], and, as it now stands, forms the best American work on the science of architecture extant." Baird advertised it for $10.00 by mail, free of postage to any part of the United States.

The copy at the University of Nebraska—Lincoln bears the elaborate signature of Louis D. Goulette.

19. ***Civil Architecture***, etc.: 1876. Reissue by Henry Carey Baird of the eleventh edition of 1870. Quarto. 191 pp.; 102 pls. "finely engraved on copper." Hitchcock 1155.

Baird did not repeat the decorative covers of earlier editions. He reverted to a plain green cloth binding with embossed frame and gold-stamped titles on the cover (CIVIL ARCHITECTURE / SHAW) and spine. As has often been pointed out, copper plates wear down after repeated impressions and need to be re-touched or re-engraved. Since the 102 plates here first appeared in 1852, and were used for reissues of 1856 and 1870, their linear crispness in this reprint suggests that they had been refreshed.

The copy at the American Antiquarian Society (ex libris Fitchburg Public Library) has the name "Thomas Mack / Boston, Mass." written on the inside front cover. Several Thomas Macks appear in the local press in the late nineteenth century, but it seems that only one had a connection to Fitchburg: the prominent dry goods merchant (1827–97) who, according to Library records, was born in that town, made his first monetary contribution to its library in 1859, and, while living at 269 Commonwealth Avenue, Boston, from 1883 to his death, donated four paintings to the same institution. The Avery Library copy is signed "John F. Hunt / May 1882 / Laredo / Tx." The Princeton University copy has a bookplate of the Elizabeth Foundation Library of the College of New Jersey, with inscribed dates 1886 and 1888.

20. **_Civil Architecture_,** etc. Reprint, 1887. Not in Hitchcock.

Of this reprint Charles B. Wood III has written that "it probably did not sell well as it was very much out of date and out of fashion." There is a copy at the Michigan Technical University bearing a stamp with the school's original name, Michigan Mining School, established in 1885.

21. **_Civil Architecture_,** etc. Reprint, 1900. Not in Hitchcock.

This reprint is listed by Online Computer Library Center (OCLC) although no copies were located for this survey.[150] As late as 1903 Baird flogged the eleventh edition in the catalogue of his books published as an advertisement in his Edward Kirk, _The Cupola Furnace._

22. **_The Modern Architect: a Classic Victorian Stylebook and Carpenter's Manual._** New York: Dover Publications, Inc., 1995. Scholarly introduction by Earle G. Shettleworth, Jr.

Afterword

Had we only Shaw's surviving drawings—surely a small portion of what he produced—or his projects for domestic buildings published in his last two architectural titles, *Rural Architecture* and *The Modern Architect*, earlier scholars of nineteenth-century Boston architecture might be forgiven for neglecting him. Although there were those of his fellow townsmen who examined his drawings for large buildings, found their planning praiseworthy, and lamented the fact that they were not erected, his surviving proposed designs, except for the Boston Athenaeum, are anything but exceptional. Some observers, like Arthur Gilman but not Thomas Gordon Smith, might think the published houses rather odd. His plates of classical details, however, found imitators from New England to the South, Midwest, Texas, and Oregon. That can be demonstrated. How much his texts impacted his far-flung readers it is impossible to quantify. His designs for country churches are quaint to our eyes, but some of his New England contemporaries found them so attractive that they copied them over and over again.

But when we turn to two surviving buildings, a private house of the 1830s and a civic building of the 1840s, we stand on different critical ground. The Thaxter house ranks among the finest on Beacon Hill. Surviving documentation details the design and execution of the building. The frontispiece is pure Grecian Revival, the interior stair a masterpiece of curvilinear form, the interior details beautifully conceived, but the masterstroke, that which tops it all off, is the belvedere from which to take the measure of all Boston, as well as its surroundings. The exterior of the Manchester Town Hall is different in kind but equal in quality, indeed, far more inventive in its original combination of civic offices and mercantile spaces as well as its integrated classical form and medieval detail. Set against Isaiah Roger's contemporary temple-form Town Hall at Quincy, Massachusetts, for example, it radiates vitality as well as an originality of combined composition and decoration. Erected in the pre-eclectic age of stylistic orthodoxy, it confused contemporary Manchester historians as to its pedigree but impressed them with its distinctiveness. They found it "peculiar" and "unique" but nonetheless "fine looking," whereas it drew unreserved later praise from Professor John Coolidge in a period when such architecture usually attracted little more than scorn from academics.

Those buildings are rooted in New England, but Shaw's publications traveled across the country. With the exception of immigrant architects, such as Benjamin Henry Latrobe, and their students like Robert Mills, American architects emerging in the period covered here began their working lives in the building trades.[151] This was true of all but one of the authors of our earliest books on architecture: Asher Benjamin, Shaw, Minard Lafever, Owen Biddle, Chester Hills, and William Brown all began careers as carpenters or masons, then evolved into architects or, in words of *The Modern Architect*, "became their own masters." Their books cover much of the same territory as his. Together with occasional instruction offered by architects like John Kutts or Solomon Willard, they represented the only "school" of architecture available before the Massachusetts Institute of Technology inaugurated the country's first academic department in 1867. The early books supplied detailed construction techniques for the novice as well as instruction on, first the Roman, then the Greek, orders basic to architectural design in the neoclassical era. Shaw alone, however, added titles solely devoted to masonry building. And Shaw's emphasis on the uses of geometric projection and shading in the presentation of designs, what one observer called "mathematical and pictorial rules," something he neglected to do in his own work, also sets his *Civil Architecture* apart from his early competitors.

All of the early architectural manuals relied heavily upon the publications of English and some Continental authors. Shaw somehow surveyed both sources as, in his own word, a "Compiler," and passed on to a broad readership much larger quantities of borrowed information than did his contemporaries, information garnered from a vast assortment of specific and general literature. He cast a wide net of second-hand information on the history of European architecture and decoration. From our point of view, he seems almost cavalier in his mining of sources acknowledged and unacknowledged.

By midcentury his later publications began to look woefully dated compared to those of authors such as A. J. Downing and A. J. Davis or Samuel Sloan. Nonetheless, reprints of *Civil Architecture* continued to appear until the end of the century, whereas the works of his earlier competitors had vanished by the end of the 1850s. Despite Arthur Gilman's dismissal of the houses Shaw published in *Rural Architecture* and *The Modern Architect*, as Talbot Hamlin noted his designs were copied in his own time, and his work also found favor in some quarters during the classical revivals of the late nineteenth and late twentieth centuries.

It should also be remembered that, as examples of architectural book binding, the publishers of Shaw's last two architectural works, *Rural Architecture* and *The Model Architect*, surpassed those produced for other authors of his generation. Although many of the books in this category appeared in plain calf bindings with simple labels on the spine, some of Shaw's were issued in thick, imposing quartos with embossed covers, gilt stamping, and marbled fore edges and endpapers, as suitable for displaying in a scholar's library as for instructing a novice designer (or, eventually, for pressing specimen flowers and ferns!). Obviously, his publishers sought a readership (or at least a collectorship) outside the field of building. Modern bibliophiles prize these books too: in good condition they now call for an elevated price on the antiquarian market.

In any condition, however, where they contain owner's signatures along with residence, date, and other marginalia, they provide the historian with valuable information about the spread and the character of Shaw's influence. Although libraries in the eastern United States seem, as expected, to have the major number of his surviving volumes, we can now more fully document that his influence fanned out from Boston to the rest of the country and into Canada. Further research in the many libraries this study could not survey would undoubtedly fill in many more details about the distribution of his works.

That Shaw's publications had an appeal for a wide variety of people is also demonstrated from what we now know by the assortment of men who owned copies of his books. Some were builders and architects, of course, who probably found use for his guidance throughout their careers, and some of their works are today listed on the National Register of Historic Places. A quarter century after the publication of *Operative Masonry*, a copy fell into the hands of the architect and civil engineer William F. Durfee, for example. As a designer and builder of iron works in Massachusetts and Michigan, Durfee produced the first Bessemer steel units in this country. There were surveyors and real estate professionals, such as Charles G. Clapp of Portland, Maine, who acquired Shaw's books, and those who bought copies when young and eventually moved on to other pursuits. Charles G. Bellamy of Kittery, Maine, began life as a builder with the second edition of Shaw's *Civil Architecture* in hand and later served in state government. This first survey of Edward Shaw's career demonstrates that his influence on the culture of the nineteenth century spread far beyond Boston and New England. The next study of the region's—and the country's—architectural history cannot fail to recognize his important contributions.

NOTES

1. For a quick review of Benjamin's career see the entry by Abbott Lowell Cummings in Adolf K. Placzek, ed., *Macmillan Encyclopedia of Architects* (New York: The Free Press, 1982), Vol. 1, 176–79.

2. The basic study remains Talbot Hamlin, *Greek Revival Architecture in America* (London: Oxford University Press, 1944).

3. For Kutts, who worked in both Philadelphia and Boston, see Roger G. Reed, "John Kutts," in *The Architects of Winchester, Massachusetts* 7 (Winchester Historical Society, 2006).

4. Allen Bernstein, "Cornelius Coolidge," *Old-Time New England* 39 (October 1948).

5. Edward F. Zimmer, "The Architectural Career of Alexander Parris," PhD diss., Ann Arbor, University of Michigan reprints, 1985, 256–57, 542–43. See also Edward Shaw, *Shaw's Civil Architecture* (Boston: John P. Jewett and Company, 1852), 118.

6. Mary N. Woods, *From Craft to Profession* (Berkeley: University of California Press, 1999), 188–89.

7. A brief outline of this study appeared in James F. O'Gorman, "From Hammer to Drafting Pen; Edward Shaw of Boston." *Nineteenth Century* 35, no. 2 (2015): 2–9.

8. James F. O'Gorman, *Isaiah Rogers* (Amherst: University of Massachusetts Press, 2015).

9. *Boston Transcript*, January 5, 1903; reproduced in *The Preservation of Park Street Church Boston* (Boston: Geo. H. Ellis, Printers, 1903), 53–56. See #11 in Chapter 3.

10. New York *Daily Advertiser*, June 2, 1794; *Connecticut Journal*, September 12, 1798; *New England Palladium*, May 9, 1806.

11. Harriette F. Farwell, *Shaw Records* (Bethel, Maine: E. C. Bowler, 1904), 56–57; Talbot Hamlin, *Greek Revival*, 164; Earle G. Shettleworth, Jr., "Edward Shaw, Architect and Author," Introduction to Shaw's *The Modern Architect* (New York: Dover Publications, 1995), v–xiv.

12. He is unmentioned in the volumes on Boston published in the 1820s to 1840s such as Abel Bowen, *Picture of Boston* (Boston: Lorenz H. Bowen, 1833) or I. S. Homans, *Sketches of Boston* (Boston: Phillips, Sampson, and Company, 1851).

13. *Boston Medical and Surgical Journal*, July 4, 1848.

14. For an alternate reading of this statement see Dell Upton, "Pattern Books and Professionalism," *Winterthur Portfolio* 16 (1984): 119. Upton's fundamental study provides the broad context in which Shaw's authorial career unfolded.

15. While working on *The Modern Architect*, he was arrested, jailed, and summarily discharged on suspicion of counterfeiting bank notes. *The Bankers' Magazine* 7 (July 1852 to June 1853): 668; *Daily National Intelligencer*, January 10, 1853; *Connecticut Courant*, February 19, 1853.

16. It is worth noticing here that the designer of the cover of the sixth edition of Shaw's *Civil Architecture* (1852), and other editions, included a composition of intertwined carpenters' tools on the spine of that book (see Figure 23). Perhaps this, too, is meant to suggest the separate roles of builder and designer.

17. "Oliver Smith, Housewright and Itinerant Architect," in *American Architects and Their Books, 1840-1915*, eds. Kenneth Hafertepe and James F. O'Gorman (Amherst: University of Massachusetts Press, 2007), 31–62. See Spiro Kostof, *America by Design* (New York: Oxford University Press, 1994), 25. According to Cavanagh, Oliver Smith, in his *The Domestic Architect* of 1852, seems to have shown a balloon frame that may be the earliest, whereas the first drawing with a precise description is found in William Bell, *Carpentry Made Easy*, 1858. Peter C. Walsh, *Woodworking Tools, 1600–1900*, 2008 (online as EB27238), Fig. 19 (1855 edition), points out the traditional design of the carpenter's dividers, and notes the presence of the balloon frame.

18. Woods, *From Craft to Profession, passim.* Upton, "Pattern Books," 122, sees this as "perhaps unconsciously . . . the architects' private image of the ideal architect–client relationship." In the Preface to his *Practice of Architecture* (1833, etc.), Benjamin wrote, "It has been too prevalent a habit, among those who would not think themselves capable of instructing a Carpenter in the Art of planning or sawing boards, or a bricklayer in laying bricks, to undertake a much more difficult task of becoming their own Architects."

19. The catalogue is available online. The list includes two Asher Benjamin titles and a few English publications on architecture, but not Shaw's *Civil Architecture*.

20. Martha J. McNamara," "Defining the Profession: Books, Libraries, and Architects," in, *American Architects and Their Books to 1848*, eds. Kenneth Hafertepe and James F. O'Gorman (Amherst: University of Massachusetts Press, 2001), 73–89.

21. Jack Quinan, "Some Aspects of the Development of the Architectural Profession in Boston between 1800 and 1830," *Old-Time New England* LXVIII (July–December 1977): 32–37.

22. One possible avenue to Harvard would have been Cornelius Coolidge, a graduate of the school.

23. See Henry-Russell Hitchcock, *American Architectural Books* (New York: Da Capo Press, 1976).

24. Michael J. Lewis, "Owen Biddle and the Young Carpenter's Assistant," in *American Architects and Their Books to 1848*, eds. Hafertepe and O'Gorman, 149–62; and Conor Lucey, "Owen Biddle and Philadelphia's Real Estate Market, 1798–1806," *Journal of the Society of Architectural Historians* 75 (March 2016): 34–38.

25. Jacob Landy, *The Architecture of Minard Lafever* (New York: Columbia University Press, 1970), Chap. II.

26. O'Gorman, *Isaiah Rogers*, 30–31.

27. Even adding other names to the list of authorities cited by Benjamin leaves him far short of Shaw. However, he did cite a few that Shaw apparently failed to mention, such as his references when discussing carpentry to Henri-Louis Duhamel du Moncreau, Jean-Baptiste Rondelet, Thomas Tredgold, and William Emerson in *The Builder's Guide*.

28. See Charles B. Wood III, "Asher Benjamin, Andrew Jackson Downing: Two Divergent Forms of Bookmaking," *American Architects and Their Books to 1848*, eds. Hafertepe and O'Gorman, 181–98.

29. For an extended discussion of Smith and his publications, see Cavanagh, "Oliver Smith," in *American Architects and Their Books, 1840 to 1915*, eds. Hefertepe and O'Gorman, 31–62. Unexpected are Smith's designs in the Turkish and Chinese styles (Pl. XLII).

30. The two men may also have had a family connection. For Moore, see the obituary in *The Historical and Genealogical Register* XXX (October 1876): 399–406. For the merger of the *Mirror* and the *Aurora*, see the *Boston Transcript*, March 8, 1834.

31. Although architects like Isaiah Rogers, William Sparrell, and A. B. Young were members of the Charitable Mechanic Association, Shaw apparently never joined.

32. *Boston Commercial Gazette*, January 25, 1827.

33. Orlando Faulkland Lewis, *The Development of American Prisons and Prison Customs* (Albany: the Prison Association of New York, 1922), 289.

34. Roger G. Reed, *Building Victorian Boston* (Amherst: University of Massachusetts Press, 2007), 62–69.

35. Caroline Wells Healey Dall, *In Memoriam: Alexander Wadsworth*, 1898; Charles A. Birnbaum and Robin Karson, eds., *Pioneers of American Landscape Design* (New York: McGraw-Hill, 2000), 420–22.

36. For a discussion of drawing at this period, see Lois Olcott Price, *Line, Shade and Shadow: The Fabrication and Preservation of Architectural Drawings* (New Castle, Delaware: Oak Knoll Press, 2010), 1–50.

37. Middlesex County Registry of Deeds, Book 316, 40–41.

38. Thelma Fleishman, *Images of America: Newton* (Newton [Massachusetts] Historical Society), 18.

39. *Boston Journal*, June 8, 1868.

40. Richard Foster Stoddard, "The Architecture and Technology of Boston Theatres, 1794–1854," PhD diss., Yale University, 1971, 144. Stoddard cites Suffolk County deeds, Book 357, 105.

41. Second edition, 1833, 209.

42. "An Index to Boston Building Contracts Recorded in the Suffolk County Registry of Deeds," four volumes, 1820 to 1849, compiled by Earle G. Shettleworth, Jr., augmented by "An Index to Building Contracts Recorded in the Middlesex County Registry of Deeds," compiled by Roger G. Reed. Copies available at Historic New England.

43. Raymond E. Barlow and Joan E. Kaiser, *The Glass Industry in Sandwich* (East Sandwich, Mass.: Barlow-Kaiser Publishing Company, 1983), 61.

44. Craig Lambert, "An Aristocrat's Killing," *Harvard Magazine* (July–August 2003): 24.

45. In 1831 Shaw made a copy of a survey by Alexander Wadsworth of a part of Chelsea, Massachusetts, across the Mystic River from Boston. It is now in the archive of Historic New England. His reason for doing so remains unknown.

46. Shettleworth, "Index to Boston Building Contracts," 1830–1839, 106. The existing 48 West Cedar Street has a façade very like that of the Pickney Street house.

47. Ferris Greenslet, *The Life of Thomas Bailey Aldrich* (Boston: Houghton, Mifflin, 1908), op. 152 (photograph of the façade).

48. *Proceedings of the Bostonian Society*, 13 January 1903, 31. "Adam Wallace Thaxter, Jr.," *Ballou's Pictorial Drawing-Room Companion*, February 28, 1857, 140, with portrait.

49. *The Bankers' Magazine*, May 1854, 918. Many previous writers about the Thaxter house have confused its commissioner with his father, a mathematical instrument maker.

50. "Enlargement of the State House, Boston," *Ballou's*, April 26, 1856.

51. Fine Arts Library, Harvard University. Thanks to Erica Hirshler for telling me of this extraordinary documentation.

52. For an excellent photographic coverage of the house in its present state see Gayle Hargreaves with photography by J. David Bohl, "Classical Furniture Graces a Greek Revival Home," *Antiques and Fine Art* (Autumn/Winter 2007): 176–88.

53. For a comparison between these specifications and those written for contemporary row houses by his younger rival, Gridley J. F. Bryant, see Reed, *Building Victorian Boston*, 35–39.

54. Some of the drawings look preliminary rather than final. There is an undated note to Thaxter in which Moulton agrees to "Build the other Storey according to Plan and Specification" for $787.25. Could this have been a change order after the March contract between them? The drawing of the façade, of course, shows the final number of stories. Shaw's itemized bill notes a series of changes to the drawings, including "making a new set of Plans on 3 March."

55. Thaxter contemplated further changes in 1856, at least in interior decoration. The file contains an apparently heretofore unremarked letter from none other

than Thomas A. Teft of Providence. The September 18th note refers to a meeting of the previous day in the receiving parlor, "and not the dining room as I was thinking when I was talking about the [illegible word] Antique," the mistake being made because they had dined in the room "at the time." This suggests a discussion about the entry floor, as does his further remark in which he does "not propose any heavy decoration—but would rather have the pilasters, architrave and cornice [of Shaw's design?] [painted] nearly white and the ground and frieze of a warm grey tint. . . . The ceiling to be a very light bluish grey. . . . If the room is decorated in this manner it will be very chaste and I think beautiful. I trust also that it will please your [keen?] critical eye." Teft included a slight colored sketch of the cornice. Whether or not this happened remains unknown. (Teft sailed for Europe in December and died there two years later.)

56. Hamlin, *Greek Revival*, 118.
57. Charles S. Parker, *Town of Arlington, Past and Present* (Arlington, Mass.: C. S. Parker & Son, 1907), 104; Richard A. Duffy, "Lost Arlington: The William W. Warren House," *Arlington Advocate* (June 6, 1986): 11A.
58. Benjamin and William R. Cutter, *History of the Town of Arlington, Massachusetts* (Boston: David Clapp & Son, 1880).
59. *Boston Daily Evening Transcript*, April 11, 1846.
60. Historic New England Library and Archives, gift of Earle G. Shettleworth, Jr. See James F. O'Gorman, ed., *Drawing Toward Home* (Boston: Historic New England, 2010), 56–57.
61. We shall find Shaw specifying a Bryant and Hermann furnace again for the David Sears house. He described and illustrated it in his *Practical Masonry* of 1846. He usually spelled "Hermann" with one "n," but published ads usually use two.
62. Keith N. Morgan, Elizabeth Hope Cushing, and Roger G. Reed, *Community by Design* (Amherst: University of Massachusetts Press, 2013), 10–12. It remains to be seen whether Shaw designed any of the other buildings the Sears family erected in the area, but as Sears seems to have favored using different architects for different buildings, perhaps he did not.
63. Shettleworth, "Edward Shaw, Architect and Author," ix. Documents cited are in the Sears Papers at the Massachusetts Historical Society.
64. Although he does not recognize it as the Sears house and cites its appearance as reprinted in *The Modern Architect*. Upton, "Pattern Books," 136 and 139, Fig. 23.
65. James F. O'Gorman, "Wm. Bailey Lang's *Highland Cottages* as Endorsed by A. J. Downing," *Nineteenth Century* 33 (Spring 2013): 28–33.
66. Historic New England Library and Archives, gift of Earle G. Shettleworth, Jr. See O'Gorman, *Drawing Toward Home*, 58–59.

67. I. C. Knowlton, *Annals of Calais, Maine*, 1875, Chapter XVII; the *Christian Register*, Boston, August 10, 1833.

68. Alice Doan Hodgson, *Orford, New Hampshire* (Orford: Historical Fact Publications, n.d.), iii and 30.

69. According to Talcott Williams, "A Brief Object-Lesson in Springfield Architecture," *American Architect and Building News* (November 12, 1881): 227. The author seems to suggest the unlikely scenario that Shaw copied his design from this church.

70. The application form for the National Register of Historic Places for the Wilbur Fiske Haven house in Malden gives George Hansen Fall as the builder of this church without citing a source.

71. "The First Methodist Church in Malden," *Malden Mirror*, October 20, 1883; Centre Methodist Episcopal Church, *Celebration of the One-Hundredth Anniversary of the Organization of the Church*, May 1–8, 1921, 25–28, with photograph.

72. In his article in the *Boston Transcript*, January 5, 1903, Thomas W. Silloway seems to say that Shaw designed the First Parish Meeting Houses of Cambridge and Watertown. Isaiah Rogers designed the one, and there is no known evidence giving the other to Shaw.

73. Harold Kirker, *The Architecture of Charles Bulfinch* (Cambridge, Mass.: Harvard University Press, 1969), 298–99; Susan E. Maycock, *East Cambridge* (Cambridge, Mass., 1988), 143–44 (with errors); Shettleworth, "Architect and Author," vii.

74. Emerson Gallery, Hamilton College, *A Neat Plain Modern Style: Philip Hooker and His Contemporaries* (Amherst: University of Massachusetts Press, 1993), 262–79.

75. *Proceedings of the Most Worshipful Grand Lodge of Ancient Free and Accepted Masons . . . 1826 to 1844*, 241.

76. *Boston Traveler*, September 7, 1832.

77. O'Gorman, *Isaiah Rogers*, 40–42.

78. Bruce Laverty, Michael J. Lewis, and Michelle Taillon Taylor, *Monument to Philanthropy* (Philadelphia: Girard College, 1998).

79. Laverty et al., *Monument to Philanthropy*, 26.

80. Richard G. Carrott, *The Egyptian Revival* (Berkeley: University of California Press, 1978), 146–92.

81. *The Portsmouth Journal of Literature and Politics*, December 21, 1839, 51.

82. See Reed, *Building Victorian Boston*, 62; and James F. O'Gorman, *Henry Austin* (Middleton, Conn.: Wesleyan University Press, 2008), 217, note 8.

83. O'Gorman, *Isaiah Rogers*, 129–35.

84. Margaret Nash De Laittre, "Ammi Burnham Young and the Construction of the Boston Custom House," master's thesis, University of Virginia, 1975),

15. De Laittre cites a letter, Shaw to Woodbury, National Archive Records Group 56, entry 99. We have also used Pamela Scott's summary of that letter sent to Earle G. Shettleworth, Jr. in 1996, which differs from De Laittre's account.

85. Rare Book Room, Boston Public Library, CAB 60.129.3, badly in need of conservation. Stuck to the reverse of the last sheet is a copy of the plate showing two plans, one section, and Hammatt Billing's perspective rendering of Young's winning design. Affixed to the inside of the rear cover is an unattributed ink and wash elevation of the Court House (?), a weaker presentation of a cruciform design with dome but without the colossal order.

86. Abbott Lowell Cummings, "The Ohio State Capitol Competition," *Journal of the Society of Architectural Historians* 12 (May 1953): 15–18.

87. Josiah Quincy, *The History of the Boston Athenaeum* (Cambridge, Mass.: Metcalf and Company, 1851); [Jane S. Knowles], *Change and Continuity: A Pictorial History of the Boston Athenaeum* (Boston: The Boston Athenaeum, 1976); Catharina Slautterback, *Designing the Boston Athenaeum* (Boston: The Athenaeum, 1999).

88. The project, now convincingly assigned to Shaw by Earle G. Shettleworth, Jr. on the basis of similar work, was attributed to Richard Bond by Janet Knowles.

89. Reed, *Building Victorian Boston*, 66–69.

90. C. E. Potter, *The History of Manchester* (Manchester, NH: C. E. Potter, 1856), 614–17.

91. Richard M. Candee, Letter to the Editor, *Journal of the Society of Architectural Historians* 39 (May 1980): 178–79.

92. John Coolidge, *Mill and Mansion* (New York: Russell & Russell, 1942), 97, 210.

93. Manchester's 1999 City Hall renovation by Lavallee/Brensinger Architects won the local People's Choice Award for Historic Preservation for the restoration of the exterior brick and granite. The exterior brickwork remains unpainted, as it was originally, despite Shaw's wishes.

94. Anyone who discusses nineteenth-century American architectural books is deeply indebted to Professor Hitchcock for his basic study of titles and editions.

95. This summary relies heavily on the following works: Michael Winship, "Manufacturing and Book Production," in Scott E. Casper et al., *History of the Book in America*, 3, eds. Scott E. Casper et al. (Chapel Hill: American Antiquarian Society, 2007), 40 ff.; Julia Miller, *Books Will Speak Plain* (Ann Arbor: Legacy Press, 2010), 141 ff.; Sue Allen and Charles Gullans, *Decorated Cloth in America: Publishers' Bindings, 1840–1910* (Los Angeles; University of California, 1994); Sue Allen, "Machine-Stamped Bookbindings, 1834–1860," *Antiques* 115 (March 1979): 564–72; and Sue Allen, *American Book*

Covers, 1830–1900; A Pictorial Guide (Washington: Library of Congress, 1998).

96. For a discussion of bookmaking in the context of architectural publications by two of Shaw's contemporaries see Charles B. Wood III, "Asher Benjamin, Andrew Jackson Downing: Two Divergent Forms of Bookmaking," in Hafertepe and O'Gorman, *American Architects and Their Books to 1848*, 181–198.

97. Review of Rexford Newcomb's *Architecture of the Old Northwest Territories* in the *William and Mary Quarterly* 8, no. 2 (April 1951): 261.

98. There is no thorough state survey such as Mary Wallace Crocker published in "Asher Benjamin: The Influence of His Handbooks on Mississippi Buildings," *Journal of the Society of Architectural Historians* 38 (October 1979): 266–70. She names some builders and designers but there is no mention of the owners of books.

99. James F. O'Gorman, "From Maine to Oregon: The Distribution of Edward Shaw's Architectural Publications," *Nineteenth Century* 36 (Spring 2016): 24–29.

100. Jhennifer A. Amundson, "'Vast Avenues to Knowledge': Thomas Ustick Walter's Books," Hafertepe and O'Gorman, *American Architects and Their Books, 1840–1915*, 63–94. Shaw's books do not appear to have been one of Walter's avenues.

101. Upton, "Pattern Books," 117–18.

102. Hamlin, *Greek Revival*, is an example of inclusion. An example of neglect is James Early's "American Architectural Writing in the Early Nineteenth Century," *Journal of Architectural Education* 12 (Summer 1957): 23–25. Dell Upton's "Pattern Books" of 1984 suggests more recent recognition.

103. See, for examples, James F. O'Gorman, "An 1886 Inventory of H. H. Richardson's Library," *Journal of the Society of Architectural Historians* 61 (May 1982): 150–55; and William A. Coles, "Richard Morris Hunt and his Library," *Art Quarterly* 30 (Fall–Winter 1967): 225–37.

104. Louis H. Gibson, *Beautiful Houses: A Study in House Building* (New York: Thomas Y. Crowell & Company, 1895), 129–31.

105. Thomas Gordon Smith, introduction to Asher Benjamin, *Practice of Architecture* (New York: Da Capo Press, 1994), Fig. 14.

106. I follow the distinction given by Fredson Bowers in the Foreword to his *Principles of Bibliographical Description*, (Princeton, NJ: Princeton University Press, 1949).

107. Here and elsewhere in this catalogue, this information comes from the copyright page, the reverse of the title page.

108. Peter Dzwonkoski, ed., *American Literary Publishing Houses, 1638–1899*, (Detroit: Gale Research Company, 1986), 239. For Lincoln, see *The New-England Magazine* IV (1833): 89.

109. Wood, "Asher Benjamin," 187.

110. James F. O'Gorman, *Three American Architects* (Chicago: University of Chicago Press, 1991), 72–74.

111. Hamlin, *Greek Revival*, 164–65.

112. O'Gorman, *Isaiah Rogers, passim.*

113. Michael Batinski, *Pastkeepers in a Small Place* (Amherst: University of Massachusetts, 2004), 191.

114. Dzwonkoski, *Publishing Houses*, 295.

115. James F. O'Gorman, *The Perspective of Anglo-American Architecture* (Philadelphia: The Athenaeum, 1995).

116. It should be noted that, despite the fact that models were in common use during his career by Isaiah Rogers and many others, Shaw does not mention them.

117. Maureen Ogle, "Domestic Reform in Household Plumbing, 1840–1870," *Winterthur Portfolio* 28 (Spring 1993): 33.

118. Susan Swiatosz, "A Technical History of Late Nineteenth Century Windows in the United States," *APT Bulletin* 17 (1985): 31–38; and Rudy R. Christian, "Conservation of Historic Building-Trades Education: A Timber Framer's View," in *APT Bulletin* 33 (2002): 39–42. See also Michael J. Pulice, "Unraveling the Benjamin Deyerle Legend: An Analysis of Mid-Nineteenth-Century Brickwork in the Roanoke Valley of Virginia," *Vernacular Architectural Forum* 12 (2005): 39.

119. Yvonne Brault Smith, *John Haley Bellamy, Carver of Eagles* (Portsmouth: Portsmouth Marine Society, 1982), *passim.* John was Charles's son.

120. John Morrill Bryan, "Boston's Granite Architecture, c. 1810–1860," PhD diss., Boston University, 1972. Newspaper ads in 1833 list a work called *Practical Masonry*, no author named, with ninety steel-plate engravings and several hundred working drawings. See the *New York Evening Post*, September 25, 1833. No such book is listed in the catalogue of the Library of Congress.

121. Compare Thomas Jefferson, *Notes on the State of Virginia*, 1787, Query XV: "A country whose buildings are of wood, can never increase in its improvements to any considerable degree. . . . Whereas when buildings are of durable materials, every new edifice is an actual and permanent acquisition to the state, adding to its value as well as its ornament."

122. *Annual Report of the Adjutant-General of the State of New York for the Year 1898*, 1248.

123. Joyce K. Bibb, "Charles O. Clapp," *A Biographical Dictionary of Architects in Maine* (Augusta: Maine Historic Preservation Commission, 1988).

124. Rossiter Johnson, ed., *The Twentieth-Century Biographical Dictionary of Notable Americans*, Vol. 111 (Boston: The Biographical Society, 1904).

125. Daniel D. Reiff, "At the Core of His Career," in Hafertepe and O'Gorman, *American Architects and Their Books, 1840–1915*, 129–48.

126. Clay Lancaster, "Adaptations from the Greek Revival Builders' Guides in Kentucky," *The Art Bulletin* 32 (March 1950: 62–70; Clay Lancaster, "Major Thomas Lewinski: Émigré Architect in Kentucky," *Journal of the Society of Architectural Historians* 11 (December 1952): 64; Clay Lancaster, *Antebellum Architecture of Kentucky* (Lexington: The University Press of Kentucky, 1991), 184–86, 296.

127. Catherine W. Bishir, "Sampson, James," "North Carolina Architects & Builders: A Biographical Dictionary," on line; *A Guide to Wilmington's African American Heritage* (Wilmington: City of Wilmington, 2013).

128. James F. O'Gorman, *Accomplished in All Departments of Art: Hammatt Billings of Boston, 1818–1874* (Amherst: University of Massachusetts Press, 1998), 44–45.

129. For comparison, see the unsigned review of Asher Benjamin's *Builder's Guide,* one by a gentler critic who also wanders far beyond the book in question, in *The North American Review*, April 1841, 41.

130. January 1843, and October 1844. None of the three articles is signed, but Gilman's touch is apparent in all.

131. For Shaw's bargeboards see Richard Klein and David A. Lipstreu, "Bargeboard Details in the Western Reserve of Ohio: 1830-1860," *Bulletin of the Association for Preservation Technology* 13 (1981): 34–37.

132. Wood, "Asher Benjamin,"181–98.

133. We might now find odd Gilman's use here of "illuminated" in a pejorative sense, as he must have intended it, but his meaning may have been related to one definition given of *illuminate* as it appears in the 1845 edition of Webster's *American Dictionary*: "One of a sect of heretics pretending to possess extraordinary light and knowledge."

134. Arthur Gilman to Richard Upjohn, April 10, 1845. Upjohn Papers, New York Public Library.

135. Hamlin, *Greek Revival*, 165.

136. Elizabeth G. Hitchcock, *Jonathan Goldsmith, Master Builder in the Western Reserve* (Cleveland: Western Reserve Historical Society, 1980).

137. Shettleworth, "Edward Shaw, Architect and Author," xii.

138. Smith, Introduction to Asher Benjamin, *Practice of Architecture*, xiv.

139. "The Greek Revival in America and Some of Its Critics," Fig. 3.

140. Dzwonkoski, *Publishing Houses*, 324.

141. Earle G. Shettleworth, Jr., "John Calvin Stevens's Architectural Library," in Hafertepe and O'Gorman, *American Architects and Their Books, 1840–1915*, 217.

142. Dzwonkoski, *Publishing Houses*, 226.

143. See Christopher P. Monkhouse, *Faneuil Hall Market: An Account of Its Many Likenesses* (Boston: Bostonian Society, 1968).
144. Prentiss Webster, ed., *The Story of the City Hall Commission* (Lowell: City Newspaper Co., 1894).
145. Deborah Thompson, *Bangor, Maine, 1769–1914, An Architectural History* (Orono: University of Maine Press, 1988), 346–50 and *passim*.
146. James Cooke Mills, *History of Saginaw County Michigan*, Vol. II (Saginaw: Seemann & Peters: 1918), 165–66, with portrait. His son, Frank E. Kirby (b. 1849), was a marine engineer and architect, *ibid.*, 166–68.
147. Cavanagh, "Oliver Smith," in Hafertepe and O'Gorman, *American Architects and Their Books to 1848*, 40.
148. Judith Wellman, ed., *Landmarks of Oswego County* (Syracuse: Syracuse University Press, 1988), 294.
149. Albert J. Von Frank, "The Secret World of Radical Publishers: The Case of Thayer and Eldridge of Boston," in *Boston Histories*, eds. James M. O'Toole and David Quigley (Boston: Northeastern University Press, 2004), 52–70.
150. Shettleworth, "Edward Shaw, Architect and Author," xi.
151. Woods, *From Craft to Profession, passim*.

Appendix
Some Authors and Books Copied from and/or Referred to in Shaw's Texts

It is obvious that in some cases Shaw knew the work of an author only in translation and at second hand. Some titles are listed below because, as a "compiler," he copied passages from them verbatim, without acknowledgment. References appear in more than one book. Dates are of first or early editions. Some guesswork was involved in compiling the list, which is, no doubt, incomplete.

CIVIL ARCHITECTURE

Henry Aldrich, *The Elements of Civil Architecture According to Vitruvius and Other Ancients*, translated by Philip Smith (1818)

Archibald Alison, *Essays on the Nature and Principles of Taste* (1821)

T. B. Armstrong, *Journal of Travels in the Seat of War, During the Last Two Campaigns of Russia and Turkey* (1831)

(probably) James Basire, *The Rudiments of Ancient Architecture* (1789), with extracts from Vitruvius, Pliny the Elder, Scamozzi, Chambers, Vivant Denon, and others; and mention of the ancients Pytheas, Tarchiesius, and Hermogenes.

The Bible

Cato (the Elder)

William Chambers, *A Treatise on the Decorative Parts of Civil Architecture* (1759)

Hewson Clarke and John Dougal, *The Cabinet of the Arts* (1817)

Diodorus Siculus, *Bibliotheca historica*, on the buildings of Palestine (in English by 1814)

Theodore Dwight, *A Journal of a Tour of Italy in the Year 1821* (1821)

[William H. Eliot], *Description of Tremont House* (1830)

James Elmes, *Lectures on Architecture* (1823)

Euclid

Gentlemen's Magazine

Nicolaus Goldmann, *Vitruvii Volute Ionica (1649)*

Joseph Gwilt, *Rudiments of Architecture* (1826); and (perhaps) *Sciography* (1822; see also *Civil Architecture*, 1852, below)

James Hall, "Essay on the Origin and Principles of Gothic Architecture," *Transactions of the Royal Society of Edinburgh* (1797). Shaw cites this but also mentions the now more familiar book version of 1813.

John Haviland, *The Builder's Assistant* (1818–21)

Bryan Higgins, *Experiments and Observations Made with the View of Improving the Art of Composing and Applying Calcereous Cements, and of Preparing Quicklime* (1780)

Robert Hooke, *Lectures de Potentia Restitutiva (1679)*

Sebastien Le Clerc, *Traité d'architecture* (1714)

John Nicholson, *The Operative Mechanic, and British Machinist* (1825); *The Builder's Practical Guide*, (1830)

Peter Nicholson, *Popular Course of Pure and Mixed Mathematics* (1822); *The Carpenter's New Guide* (1808); *Principles of Architecture* (1809); (probably) *Architectural Dictionary* (1812–19); *Rudiments of Practical Perspective* (1822); *Practical Masonry* (1830; see also *Practical Masonry*, below)

Andrea Palladio, *I quarto libri dell'archittetura* (1570), many translations

Charles Frederick Partington, *The Builder's Complete Guide* (1825)

Pausanias

Claude Perrault, *Ordonnance des cinq espèces de colonnes selon la méthode des anciens* (1683). There were a number of translations, but Shaw cites the French title.

The Works of Alexander Pope (1752)

Hieranymous Pradus, see Villapandus

Willey Reveley (see James Stuart)

Nicholas Revett (see James Stuart)

Vincenzo Scamozzi, *L'idea dell'architettura universale* (1615)

John Smeaton, *A Narrative of the Building and a Description of the Construction of the Edystone Lighthouse* (1792)

James Stuart (with Nicolas Revett and Willey Reveley), *The Antiquities of Athens and Other Monuments of Greece* (1762–95)

James Thomson, "Liberty" (poem, 1735–36)

Ithiel Town, *A Description of Ithiel Town's Improvement in the Construction of Wood and Iron Bridges* (1821)

Giacomo Barozzi da Vignola, *Regola delli cinque ordini d'architettura* (1562)

Villapandus: (Hieronymous Pradus and Joannus Baptista Villapandus), *In Ezechielem Explanationes et Apparatus Urbis* (1596–1605)

Vitruvius, *De Architectura* (many editions and translations)

Dominique Vivant, Baron Denon, (a.k.a. Vivant Denon), *Travels in Upper and Lower Égypt* (1802)

John Wood, *A Dissertation upon the Orders of Columns, and Their Appendages* (1750)

CIVIL ARCHITECTURE, 1852

(These probably stem from Silloway and Harding, who "revised and improved" this title in this edition.)

John Britton, *Cathedral Antiquities of England* (1814–36)

James Dallaway, *A Series of Discourses upon Architecture in England* (1833)

Joseph Gwilt, (probably) *An Encyclopaedia of Architecture* (1842)

George Millers, *Description of the Cathedral Church of Ely* (1808)

John Henry Parker, (probably) *Introduction to the Study of Gothic Architecture* (1849)

Augustus Charles Pugin, (probably) *Specimens of Gothic Architecture* (1821–23)

OPERATIVE MASONRY

Torbern Olof Bergman (perhaps), *Essays, Physical and Chemical* (1779–81)

The Cyclopaedia; or, Universal Dictionary of Arts, Sciences, and Literature (1819–20)

Robert Doffie, *Memoirs of Agriculture, and other Oeconomical Arts* (1771)

Alberto Fortis, *Viaggio in Dalmazia* (1778)

Samuel Frederick Gray, *Operative Chemistry* (1828)

Frederick Hall, (probably) *Catalogue of Minerals Found in the State of Vermont,* (1824)

Antoine-Joseph Loriot, *Mémoire sur une découverte dans l'art de Bâtire ... La méthode de compser un Ciment ou Mortier* (1774)

Benjamin Thompson, Count Rumford, *The Complete Works* (several editions)

RURAL ARCHITECTURE AND THE MODERN ARCHITECT

Edmund Aikin, *Essay on the Doric Order* (1810)

Jacques-François Blondell (perhaps), *Cours d'architecture* (1771–77)

(?) Henry Bromley (a.k.a. Anthony Wilson), *A Catalogue of Engraved British Portraits* (1793)

Samuel H. Brooks, *Designs for Cottage and Villa Architecture* (1839)

William Bullock, *Six Months' Residence and Travels in Mexico* (1824)

Roland Fréart de Chambray, *Parallèle de l'architecture antique avec la modern* (1650)

Joseph Gwilt, *Encyclopaedia of Architecture* (1842)

William Martin Leake, *Topography of Athens* (1821)

(John?) Mitford on James Gibbs or Lord Burlington (source unknown)

Thomas Rickman, *An Attempt to Discriminate the Styles of English Architecture* (1817)

Walter Scott, "The Lay of the Last Minstrel" (poem, 1805)

Anthony Wilson (see Henry Bromley)

PRACTICAL MASONRY

David Booth, *The Art of Brewing* (1829)

Martin Heinrich Klaproth, *Beiträge zur Cemischen Kenntniss der Mineralköper (1795–1810)*

Peter Nicholson, *Practical Masonry, Bricklaying, and Plastering* (1830)

(perhaps) Wyatt Papworth, ed., *Dictionary of Architecture* (1853)

Arthur L. Porter, *The Chemistry of the Arts; being a Practical Display of the Arts and Manufactures which Depend on Chemical Principles* (1830)

Mary Strickland, *A Memoir of the Life, Writings, and Mechanical Inventions of Edmund Cartwright* (1843)

Louis Nicolas Vauquelin (perhaps), *Dictionnaire de chimie et de métallurgie* (1815)

Index

— Index —

(Shaw, his buildings, and his books appear throughout the text. They are not listed here.)

149

www.ingramcontent.com/pod-product-compliance
Lightning Source LLC
Chambersburg PA
CBHW080926100426
42812CB00007B/2385